HOW TO MANIPULATE
THE MANIPULATOR

A Guide to Winning the War against
Deceitful Individuals

Saoud Al Mualla

authorHOUSE®

AuthorHouse™ UK Ltd.
500 Avebury Boulevard
Central Milton Keynes, MK9 2BE
www.authorhouse.co.uk
Phone: 08001974150

First published by AuthorHouse 10/23/2009

ISBN: 978-1-4490-2938-8 (e)
ISBN: 978-1-4490-2937-1 (sc)

This book is printed on acid-free paper.

For every manipulative, malicious and narcissistic person
I have met in my life: Thank you for making me wiser,
less naive and more kind as a human being.

Contents

PART I Manipulation - Fundamental Concepts   v

Introduction   1

Goals of this Handbook   5

New Philosophies for a Changing Time   7

War or Game?   10

Complexity versus Simplicity   13

The Good, the Bad and the Ugly   15

Inside the Mind of a Manipulator – *The Bad*   *17*

Ethics and Morality   23

PART II The Manipulation Plan (17 Strategic Components)   27

A Prelude   29

2. Flourish a Fight and Thrive on Adversity   37

3. Do Not "Hit with all your Might."
Be Calm as Time is Your Ally   39

4. Learn Not to Worry, Confront your Fears
and Replace Unhelpful Beliefs   44

5. Listen More, Talk Less and Never Interrupt   49

6. Rumours and Gossip   54

7. Doubt   57

8. Select your Targets Carefully and One at A Time   61

9. Underestimation   64

10. Provoking Emotions in an Opponent is A Primary Target   68

11. Fear   74

12. Anticipation and Predictability   77

13. Use Stealth and be Invisible   82

14. Trust No One   86

15. Prepare for Deception   90

16. Know When to Stop, Redefine Failure and Learn
from it to Move Forward   94

17. Enlisting the Services of *Unaware* Devoted Allies   97

18. Relaxation and Stress   102

In Conclusion   **107**

References   111

PART I
Manipulation - Fundamental Concepts

Introduction

Manipulate (verb) ORIGIN from Latin *maniples* 'handful':

1. Handle or control with dexterity (skill in performing tasks).

2. Control or influence cleverly or unscrupulously.

3. Alter or present (data) so as to mislead.

"Men are so simple and yield so readily to the desires of the
moment that he who will trick will always find another who
will suffer to be tricked."

-Niccolò Machiavelli

"For to win one hundred victories in one hundred battles is
not the acme of skill. To subdue the enemy without fighting
is the acme of skill."

-Sun Tzu

I have deliberately elected to start this handbook with definitions of
the word manipulate followed by quotations from the great masters
of manipulation: Niccolò Machiavelli *(The Prince)* and Sun Tzu
(The Art of War). In my opinion the two constitute essential starting
fundamentals to the understanding of the art of manipulation.

In today's modern and highly competitive world, we are constantly
"at war" with others, including individuals, a group or even an
organisation. The battlefield could be in a company, firm, political
arena or an office, with manipulation being the weapon of choice.

The outdated concept – of strength in numbers and artillery is the key to victory – is no longer applicable in our modern world. "Ten soldiers wisely led will beat a hundred without a head," as Euripides said. Nowadays, the key to winning is in robust planning through acquiring knowledge which eventually equips you with the advantages to win over your potential opponent(s). Throughout history, philosophers, politicians and military leaders have written infinite words on how to win wars, and about the importance of tactics, planning and thinking rather than unfocused strength and/ or numbers:

"In war, numbers alone confer no advantage.
Do not advance relying on sheer military power."
-Sun Tzu.

In fact, in this modern epoch, you can wage a war on your own (by yourself), which is one of the main points of this handbook.

Almost all politicians, generals, CEO's and leaders in many fields have come across the work of Machiavelli and the quotations of Sun Tzu, Napoleon and Winston Churchill to name a few. Although these works of geniuses are still useful to a certain extent today (in fact they will be used in the beginning of each strategy in this book), our world has evolved and those texts and tactics of the past are no longer enough; some have to be modified to suit our current time, while others have become obsolete and can no longer act as a guide in today's treacherous, competitive environment.

We have moved forward in many fields such as science, psychology, politics, economy and technology, so it is no wonder we need to update and modify our strategies, create new ones and abandon old ones.
Even if you are the best archer in the world, you will not stand a chance against a guy with a fully automatic weapon or a *Kalashnikov*. If you were the best accountant 10 years ago and still rely on a calculator

then even with all your experience you stand little chance against a novice who uses the latest computer accounting software.

I could go on giving similar examples, but the common theme is the same. To be ahead in the game – in this case war – you need to modernise and use every available piece of knowledge from every field. Be flexible and open to new ideas and tactics, think outside the box – lateral thinking – and most importantly use every means available at your disposal to win the battle.

If you look at our world today and the stories of failure in war (Vietnam, Somalia, Iraq), and businesses (Enron, GM), the common theme is these organisations did not adapt fast enough, used a poor strategy and underestimated the task. They became complacent and inflexible, or hired the wrong type of leaders. But the most common reason for failure of organisations and individuals alike is an underlying theme, which is poor planning. *The bottom line*, which sums up the reason behind failures, is that poor planning (strategies) will lose wars.

Goals of this Handbook

This handbook addresses two key issues. The first issue is to recognize *bad/devious/ malicious/deceitful* individuals. Our focus will be to acquire an understanding of their mind-set, behaviour, emotions, tactics, strengths and weaknesses. Secondly, the handbook will concentrate on the strategies and tactics capable to defeat and breakdown these characters.

The use of the words such as bad/devious/malicious/deceitful individuals will become apparent as we discuss the topic in further details. Seeking simplicity, we will group these descriptive words under the term *manipulators*. Nevertheless, these words will be used frequently throughout the book.

The strategies proposed in this handbook, are diverse, being drawn from psychology, philosophy, history, business, technology, spirituality, politics, military, sociology and science. I strongly believe that the era of speciality (i.e. knowledge in one area, for example, politics) is an obstacle for any person or group trying to progress in any modern field. This is the era of diversity in knowledge, lateral thinking and innovation. If you do not accept this philosophy, then in my view, you will be left behind in the game, playing second fiddle and concepts of triumph, success and winning should not be in your vocabulary.

The main philosophy to achieve the goals of this book is simple. No matter if you are dealing with a manipulative person or groups in any field, whether it be political, commercial or even academic, the objective is to plan by focusing your attacks on the primary (key) target (a leader, a CEO, a school principal) with the aim to break them down. Manipulation is a game of chess and once you checkmate the king, the game is over and the victory is yours.

The reader should not be put off by the words *strategy* or *war* as these words – to a certain extent – are used loosely in this book. You don't have to hold an MBA or be an expert in strategic planning nor are you expected to be a war historian. No matter what your background is, the tactics and strategies employed in this book are meant to be practical, accessible, make common sense, and most importantly, be practical (*they get results!*).

New Philosophies for a Changing Time

"Progress should mean that we are always
changing the world to fit the vision."
-G. K. Chesterton

I am sure that most of you have read many books on how to win wars (many kinds and any kind of war). A lot of you also may have noticed that those that are still famous and influential were written centuries ago, for example, Niccolò Machiavelli's *The Prince*, or Sun Tzu's *The Art of War*. Most of the so-called power figures in many fields, especially those involving intense competition (e.g. business, politics and even modern sports) have these books as their Bible. For them it is "a must read" material because they get told so by their mentors, successful predecessors or teachers. We human beings love to model or imitate others and if we are impressed by someone we emulate them. The same applies to *leaders* in any sphere of influence.

Well, here is where you will be surprised to know that I totally disagree with this outdated approach. The Iraq War, which I will use as an example throughout this is book, is a good example of using outdated tactics. Time changes, humans evolve, knowledge expands and the world is more dynamic and unpredictable than ever before. A fine example is the field of Medicine, where some studies have estimated that if a physician does not read at least four or five studies or articles per week — relating to their speciality — they will likely lose their ability to practice effectively within eight months.

Society's structure has also changed. We, in modern times, are individualistic creatures, more so than any other time in history. Most of us are egocentric or self-centred. Some of us think that we are leaders whether we want to admit it or not; it is the norm rather than the exception. This is almost a complete reversal of society's attitude of centuries ago.

So what does that mean? Simply, that rules have changed. Old books, tactics, manoeuvres and strategies are okay to read – after all, we owe it to ourselves to learn from history – but sometimes they are no longer enough, or applicable for our modern competitive society. If you choose to follow them blindly, then you will be lagging behind your opponents.

Just think about it. Almost every power hungry manipulative individual has already read or came across the work, tactics, opinions of Machiavelli, Sun Tzu, Napoleon, Alexander the Great, etc. If you also did the same, then you already share a common knowledge with this manipulative person. Let us now assume that both of you wage a war against each other. If you apply the strategies and tactics you have acquired with rigidity and inflexibility against your manipulative opponent then do not expect a strategic advantage. Worse still, if your foe is flexible and open to modifying their strategy, then the likely outcome is your imminent demise. For example in the past, the tactics of quick actions were desired – especially in a long term conflicts – whereas nowadays, subtlety and patience are more effective most of the time.

This point is crucial, as it means that we need to adapt to the new structure in society and be ahead of the game. Follow Niccolò Machiavelli or Sun Tzu blindly if you must, but believe me, high up, when you're battling with the sharks, it will be a disadvantage. You will be an open book and an easy prey, as your foe will already be familiar with your tactical knowledge. So you can stick to driving a reliable 1934 Aston Martin *Le Mans* classic automobile, which may go all the way, but you won't win the race against the modern Aston Martin V12 Vanquish 2009.

Today, people are more sophisticated, knowledgeable and educated compared to centuries ago when only a privileged few had these attributes and advantages. Nevertheless, even with their *modernisation,* today's publics are still *human beings*. So, *superficially* we may appear modernised but *deep inside*, "When push comes to shove," we are still governed by our basic instincts .The importance of this will hopefully become clearer once we discuss types of personality.

As I said previously – and I am going to repeat it for the sake of emphasis – we have evolved. We in the industrialised world are individualistic and self-centred, with a sense of self-entitlement. No longer do the majority of people consider themselves "sheep." To the contrary, almost everyone thinks they are, or deserve to be, "shapers." I am not saying that this is necessarily true in reality, as I think that *true* leaders or shapers are still few and a rare breed. But what *really* counts nowadays are society and people's beliefs, even if it is not the case. This means that in our present time, when it comes to clashes or conflicts in highly competitive environments, expect the number of your opponents, who deem themselves *leaders*, to be relatively high. This is a vital point to reflect on when building your strategy.

The message is clear: be flexible, modernise, adapt, integrate, evolve, be open to new ideas, and above all, realise that because the rules of today's war keep changing at an incredible pace, so should your strategies and tactics.

War or Game?

Many authority figures and strategists love to divide their plans and tactics into warfare against individuals, teams or organisations, into defensive and offensive tactics and so on. Call me a radical, but personally I do not think the use of the word *war* is helpful in the context of an individual's conflict. Psychologically, it creates tension, a sense of urgency and turmoil, as well as possibly becoming your worst enemy, fear. So, despite the use of the word *war* here, mentally – if you prefer – you can to substitute it for a word, such as *game*.

War may be useful in triggering immediate intense emotions. Remember the famous scene from *Braveheart*, when Mel Gibson gives his stirring speech to the troops before the battle. It is excellent to biologically trigger a fight response, an adrenaline rush; but this is unsustainable, and again, biologically speaking, a continuous prolonged adrenaline rush will exhaust you to the point of death!

On the other hand, a word like game does not have as strong an impact in the short term by inducing a similar adrenaline rush. This is a good thing in this era, where patience is a virtue and "shock and awe" is a really bad idea (but don't tell that to former U.S. President George W.Bush!).

Personally, I *favour* using the word game, because psychologically, it has a positive connotation compared to war. Nevertheless, in this book I will use the words *game, war, battle* and *conflict*. From our point of view and for the sake of simplicity in the context of this handbook, they all mean the same.

Remember, *let us evolve* and this is one step towards that. Everything counts, so a phrase or a word matters. That being said, almost all the famous quotations used in this handbook include the word *war*; and I will, in a way, contradict myself by also using it throughout! I will leave the use of whichever reference is preferable, up to you. Whether it is *war, game* or *conflict*, what matters is that you should feel comfortable with it.

So if, like me, the term *game* is your preferred choice, then please cross over the word *war* whenever you come across it and substitute it by the word *game* or, for that matter, any terminology that makes you comfortable and calm.

As for the splitting up of strategies and tactics into many categories such as offensive, defensive, unconventional, organisational and other endless classifications, I feel that it generates confusion and consumes too much mental energy. This is not a military handbook and the separation is unhelpful, so I urge you to abandon it and use one holistic approach to all of these divisions.

We may wish that we could compartmentalise strategies into neat groups, but the reality is different. Nowadays, more than ever before, in real life situations, all these artificial divisions are interrelated and don't fit neatly into categories. They may all operate at the same time, so using a compartmentalised model is unhelpful in this modern, sophisticated and fast-paced era. More crucially, the divisions may act as a hindrance in achieving our main goals in the war of manipulation.

Complexity versus Simplicity

"The simplification of anything is always sensational."
-G. K. Chesterton

"Truth is ever to be found in the simplicity and not in the multiplicity and confusion of things."
-Sir Isaac Newton

Another word that many strategists, politicians, experts and people in general use is *complexity*, as in "it is a complex issue." I would implore you to notice when this word is used and in which context and situation. Look carefully and you will notice a common theme underlying its use. When individuals or groups are at a loss or incapable of coming up with a solution or answer, are unable to adapt, or have a fear of failure, the word complex will usually pop up. Witness this tactic the next time you hear a politician answer a question they are clueless about! I'll bet you the word *complex* will come up in their response.

Well, here is my belief: *complexity* is a word we create when we are out of resources, ideas, are baffled and have no clue about what to do. The word *complexity* is extremely harmful. It makes you appear weak, unfocused and creates self-doubt. More importantly, the word gives your opponent a moral and strategic advantage over you. So, never use this dreadful word in front of a potential opponent or in a situation where you want to give the impression that you know what you are doing and that your mind is clear, focused and able to cope with whatever comes your way.

The alternative or solution to the *complexity* dilemma is simple: *simplicity*! Behind whatever we label "complex" are many layers of breakable problems or components. So the solution is to break down this complexity into its individual components, which are many simple problems. Henry Ford once said, "Nothing is particularly hard if you divide it into small jobs." So learn to prioritise the simple problems, find a solution to each and the result is your complex problem is resolved. (*Complex problem = the sum of simple problems.*)

No matter how "complex the issue is," I can assure you that with calmness, clear focus and simple approach, it can be resolved. Simplicity is an asset and one should not be offended if told that they have a simple rather than a complex outlook. In our world today, the majority of people have a complex (i.e. muddled) mind therefore finding a person with a simple (i.e. clear) mind is exceptional.

So the lesson is : every problem, no matter how *major* or *complex* it may appear to be, has an underlying structure featuring simple components which, if prioritised and resolved, will cause the complexity to vanish. The bottom line is that simplicity is a good thing and a powerful weapon if used in the right way. Let your opponent enjoy being labelled a *complex intellectual* individual, while you stick to being the *simple-minded* person.

The Good, the Bad and the Ugly

"The belief in a supernatural source of evil is not necessary;
men alone are quite capable of every wickedness."
-Joseph Conrad

"Them meaning of good and bad, of better and worse, is
simply helping or hurting."
-Ralph Waldo Emerson

People at the top or in a position of power or influence, for the sake of simplicity (remember, that is a good thing!), can be divided into two types. The first type – which is rare – is good, honest, straightforward and fair people. Now, by a process of natural selection and survival of the fittest, a person who fits into this category will rarely reach a high position because the modern-day power ladder requires certain actions and characteristics which, ideologically, are not compatible with individuals with decent, nice, candid principles. Naturally, this first group is awfully rare to come across. Some may even argue that it does not exist. So finding this group on the top of the leading, high-ranking and influential positions is exceptionally uncommon.

Now, let us move to the second type, which is far more common. This group constitutes the majority of people in positions of power in all walks of life. Natural selection and survival of the fittest is at work here, again. To reach the highest places, these people must deceive, back stab, abuse power, have little remorse, plus own other nasty features that allow them to crush and manipulate opponents to reach their goals by any means. They are *Machiavellians*; the end justifies the means – which, by the way, is a statement I totally agree with but with a little modification in the phrasing. We will be further discussing this point later on.

The best examples of the second group are manipulative politicians: being decent and honest will get them nowhere. They must lie (the phrase they use is "being economical with the truth"), and forge alliances with individuals or groups with different ideologies, who, as long as they have influence and resources (e.g. lobbyists), which could help them, attain their goals, are welcomed to "offer their assistance." They are experts in eliminating potential opponents or tarnishing their reputation. This reaches its highest intensity as elections loom. These are just a few tactics amongst many more that our modern democratically elected leaders put to full use.

The late President Richard Nixon is the modern archetypal politician who belongs to the second group. But to be fair to him, there are far worse politicians than he was. His only problem is that he got caught! Or, more accurately, employed the *wrong* tactics and strategies that *made him* get caught.

Inside the Mind of a Manipulator – *The Bad*

"If ignorant both of your enemy and yourself,
you are certain to be in peril."
-Sun Tzu

"Understanding does not cure evil, but it is a definite help,
inasmuch as one can cope with a comprehensible darkness."
-Carl Jung

"A man is but the product of his thoughts.
What he thinks, he becomes."
-Mahatma Gandhi

From the previous simplified division of people, one would guess that it is easier to manipulate or break down the first group (*the good*), right? Wrong. It is far easier to do it to the second group (*the bad and the ugly* — the devious manipulator) than the first one.

Here is where a simple understanding of human psychology offers an explanation. Predictability is the key word. The first group (*the good*), like you and I, tend to be unpredictable hence it is hard to anticipate their behaviour. Their personality is flexible, not rigid, and does not cause problems to people around them. In psychological terms, they have a healthy "normal personality."

The psychology of the second group (*the bad* — the manipulator) is totally different. Most importantly, it is predictable and that is *the key* to manipulating or breaking them down. Their personality tends to be enduring, pervasive with persistent behavioural traits across different situations. They tend to cause suffering to those around them ("Step in my way and I will crush you"). In psychology, the term used is "Personality Disorder" or "Personality Maladaptive Traits."

These individuals tend to have what we call "narcissistic personality types" amongst other types (e.g. antisocial, borderline), but this one, (i.e. the narcissistic) tends to be the *prevalent* one in our power-hungry, manipulative, remorseless individual. It is characterised by the following:

1. A grandiose sense of self-importance (e.g. exaggerates achievements and talents; expects to be recognised as superior without commensurate achievements).

2. Preoccupation with fantasies of unlimited success, power, brilliance and beauty.

3. Ingrained beliefs that he or she is "special" and unique and can only be understood by, or should be associated with, people of special or high-status.

4. A constant need for excessive admiration.

5. A sense of entitlement (i.e. favourable treatment or compliance with their expectations).

6. Being interpersonally exploitative (i.e. taking advantage of others to achieve their goals).

7. Lacking of empathy and unwillingness to recognise or identify with the feelings and needs of others.

8. Being envious of others or believing that others are envious of them.

9. Showing arrogant behaviour or attitude.

Almost one percent of the population has the full blown "disorder." However, most narcissists, and usually the ones who are in a position of power, tend to have some of the features, or have the features in a *diluted* form; as the *full blown* type or "disordered" could rarely get along in life without being exposed early on and usually do not reach their goals because of the prominence of their "disorder." But, as with everything in life, there are exceptions when these "disordered" individuals have reached the highest positions, for example, Saddam Hussain, Edi Amin, Adolf Hitler, to name but a few.

Our focus will be on the *mild* or *diluted* type of narcissist as they are more likely to succeed and are far more common to encounter since they appear in all walks of life. More importantly, this group tends to be able to control its traits as the situation requires, but only for a limited time, as their true nature will eventually appear. This means that they can do extremely well in superficial relationships, situations and even appear charming and charismatic, but they do particularly poorly in deeper and emotional relationships unless they choose partners, allies or friends who are extremely passive or even masochistic (i.e. enjoy being aggressively controlled). These passive types can be a single individual, a group, an organisation or even a whole nation.

I would not be surprised if, upon reading the above narcissistic characteristics list, many of you realised that you have had the misfortune of encountering someone with these traits. In general, they usually leave unpleasant impressions once you get to know them for a sufficient period of time. Deceivably, the initial or short term impression could be favourable, as I have mentioned that the *diluted* narcissistic individuals are usually master manipulators. They can even be extremely charming and charismatic, but only if they are known superficially or for a short period. Eventually, they will uncover or drop their mask and their true persona will rear its ugly head.

Examples that will be familiar to most are the rude, moody boss (usually branded as the "Little Hitler" by his staff); the arrogant senior colleague full of envy toward anyone who does well at work; the exploitative friend who only gets in touch if they need a favour and then disappears until the next favour is required; the cruel, unfaithful partner who has no sense of remorse; and the envious co-worker with a sense of unwarranted entitlement. One common theme linking these individuals together is that they cause misery, harm and suffering to others, especially once they become known for a sufficient period, or once the mask is uncovered and their true personality is revealed. The harm could be delivered in either a direct way (e.g. by being a boss), or an indirectly one (e.g. through being a politician).

The good news is that, surprisingly, unlike the first "normal" group, the second group (the narcissistic/bad/manipulative) can be predictable and is therefore strategically *manageable*. The bad news is that we are, to some degree, to blame for their apparent and continuous success. How? 1. By being worried of them and allowing them, because of their intimidating and manipulative tactics, "to get away with murder." 2. By paying them too much respect because they are of a higher status. 3. By fearing them. 4. By trying to please them to avoid their wrath. 5. By being passive, as Edmund Burke said, "The only thing necessary for the triumph of evil is for good men to do nothing." *All these things* we do (or don't do) tend to make the narcissist stronger.

Imagine that the narcissist has built a wall around themselves. Our appeasing or passive actions mentioned above will tend to strengthen this wall and with each person a narcissist breaks, crushes, humiliates or degrades, thus the wall becomes even stronger.

Examples from the past are plenty. Think of dictators throughout history: Hitler, Mussolini, and Saddam Hussein. We, as people played a huge part in their rise. It is impossible for one person to control a whole nation unless there is the suitable ground to do so, and whether we wish to admit it or not, we are collectively responsible for the creation and rise of those *ghastly* figures. As Martin Luther King Jr. said, "He who passively accepts evil is as much involved in it as he who helps to perpetrate it. He who accepts evil without protesting against it is really cooperating with it."

These kinds of people appear charismatic, intimidating and powerful and we, as "normal" human beings, judge them by looking at the surface. We are also governed by our emotions, and fear is one of the most powerful built-in emotions that there is. From an evolutionary prospective, when we are fearful we retreat and become submissive, and in doing so supply the necessary ammunition and fertile ground for a narcissist to rise and flourish. In the Strategy Section (Part II), we will elaborate on this by attempting to comprehend it and make use of it to our advantage.

One has to grasp that, unlike "normal" people, these individuals thrive on putting people down, crushing and humiliating potential opponents and being "victorious." All of this is because they *lack true remorse*. Even if they show remorse, it is only an act to gain an advantage. President Clinton's testimony in the Monica Lewinski affair is a good case in point.

So, unlike you and me, with the narcissist *guilt is not there*, and cruel actions act as a self-esteem builder. In fact, this individual's self-worth is built on superficial matters and on crushing and defeating opponents. They have no inner ingrained confidence or true self-esteem, and that is why they do what they do – to boost their fragile confidence. Do not be fooled by their superficial self-assurance and confident manners no matter how convincing it may appear. It is all a façade.

The narcissist lives a double life, with the outside, false personality appearing confident and even charming while the true inner personality is ugly, lacks self-confidence and is full of envy and hatred. A brilliant example from literature is in the novel, *The Picture of Dorian Gray*, by the great Oscar Wilde. The character, Dorian Gray was the false attractive person whom people see while the aging, ugly portrait hidden away from view is Dorian Gray's true narcissistic self. Another example is the novel, *Strange Case of Dr Jekyll and Mr. Hyde*, by Robert Louis Stevenson.

But what is important about knowing that a narcissist has a fragile self-confidence? The answer is that this knowledge has a great practical application in fighting and manipulating them. It is because one small set-back (a rejection, or a failure) would shatter their self esteem, and revert these individuals to almost a childlike state, in the form of shouting, acting out and even having temper tantrums (for some of you, the image of your boss, under stress, screaming like a child may come to mind!). Once again, it is our own fault that we don't push them to their limit, because we are scared and they tend to be, and actually are, scary, terrifying and intimidating individuals. The ones people always mention in terms of "you don't want to mess with THAT guy!"

Even if we do confront the narcissist, their exaggerated response, such as ear-splitting shouts and thundering threats, are enough to make us back down, especially as these people tend to be in a position of higher authority than us.

The above elaborated discussion is of supreme importance in understanding how (bad/ narcissistic/manipulative) people's minds work. As they say, "Knowledge is power," and in this case, it is the foundation of our goal, which is how to discreetly and subtly manipulate, control or break them down (i.e. manipulate the manipulator).

The good news is that if you understand the above facts about these narcissistic individuals, then you are ready to manipulate and break them down by using the strategic steps mentioned later in this book about how to wage a *silent/cold war* against them – or, if you prefer, playing a *game* with them.

Ethics and Morality

"Morality, like art, means drawing a line someplace."
-Oscar Wilde

"Ethical obligation has to subordinate itself
to the totalitarian nature of war."
-Karl Brandt

Before we discuss the strategies and tactics that are employed in waging war against a manipulative opponent, it is important to touch briefly on the issue of the ethics and morality of this war.

No matter what "experts" in ethics say, the fact remains that ethics and morality are rules dictated to us by human beings, or interpreted from a religious, philosophical, spiritual doctrine. Ethics are not written in stone. What is ethical from the point of view of one person may be unethical for another (e.g. abortion, capital punishment, euthanasia, war). Also, ethics change with time and are influenced by many factors such as religion. In medieval time, burning witches was considered a moral obligation by the church.

The situation is another factor where ethics would be dependent on the setting. An excellent example is the modification of Machiavelli's quote by the Nobel Laureate, Fredrich August von Hayek, who said, "The principle that the end justifies the means is in individualist ethics regarded as the denial of all morals. In collectivist ethics it becomes necessarily the supreme rule." This again, demonstrates how an action could be extremely immoral in one setting and completely the opposite in a different one.

I stated my own take on Machiavelli's belief, "the end justifies the means," in the introduction and mentioned that I totally agree with it. However, I followed that with the statement, "with a little modification in the phrasing." I did not elaborate on the last statement then, but I feel that now is a good time to do so.

I believe that if the end is noble and justified, then I have no guilt or remorse in using tactics to manipulate a deceitful person. So, from my point of view, the modified version of Machiavelli's quote becomes "the end justifies the means, as long as the end is noble." For example, in an organisation, if a leader is causing a great deal of misery and harm to the people around him or her, then I believe it is justifiable and even an ethical duty to use my skills in manipulation to break down that person for the collective good of the organisation and the suffering individuals in it.

The above shows how a simple statement: "the end justifies the means," could be considered ultimately immoral by many people; moral with modification by the author; or both or neither, depending on the aim, by Laureate Fredrich August von Hayek. These examples reiterate how morality and ethics are a matter of perspective and personal belief and it is not a straightforward issue.

So now we come to the ethics of our objective, which is breaking down and manipulating. It is my strong belief that each person owes it to themselves to think and reflect on their actions and whether what they do is ethical or unethical. This objective can only be reached as a result of the individual's knowledge, beliefs, experience and soul-searching. The famous French philosopher Voltaire once said, "I know many books which have bored their readers, but I know of none which has done real evil."

I must stress that my personal ethics regarding the goal of this book are my own. It is extremely important from my point of view for the reader to realise that I do not wish to force my personal ethics and views upon them. I am also a believer that human beings have a free will to make their own decisions. It is not up to me to "draw the line" between what's right/ethical and what's wrong/unethical. The views, opinions and strategies in this book are my own, based on my knowledge – factual and personal – and my experience – professional and personal.

In summary, the reader has their own ethics and morality and in all honesty I do not feel that reading this book will change the core beliefs of that person. Also, I made it clear that although the strategic approaches may work on *good* people, they are far more effective on *bad/* manipulative ones. For the purpose of achieving the desired goal of this book, the reader has to "draw the line" themselves on this issue. If they do not, then this will create doubt, confusion and moral struggle within oneself. As we will discuss later, doubt is one of your worst enemies during the battle and will likely lead to failure if it is not resolved prior to the conflict.

PART II
The Manipulation Plan
(17 Strategic Components)

A Prelude

Even though I have attempted to make this handbook simple and accessible to everyone, the fact still remains that the subject matter deals with a sophisticated, usually intelligent human being, group or organisation. Therefore, please do not be put off by certain terms and approaches and, most importantly, do not anticipate difficulties. The objective is to deal with individuals with all their uniqueness, past experiences, characteristics, behaviour and unpredictability (or predictability). So, be patient and remember that the word *complexity* is not in our vocabulary.

Throughout this handbook, I will be referring to approaching your enemy directly or indirectly. What I mean by the direct way is basically for you, yourself, to apply the tactic, whereas the indirect way is for you to use others to target your opponent.

It is important for you to understand that in both ways, you must remain anonymous. So do not confuse the direct way with direct confrontation or making your opponent aware that you have initiated a tactic (i.e. by being visible). An example of the direct way is by planting a note, giving a vague statement or sending an anonymous email or announcement; all of which is targeting your enemy.

The indirect way is straightforward and it means making others "do the dirty work," or using a third party. The best example is spreading a rumour, or inducing the third party to act on your behalf by triggering their negative emotions such as anger toward your opponent. Hopefully, these fundamental points will become clearer once we discuss each component separately.

Another point to consider is that many of the approaches share common ground and are interrelated. So although I understand that we would like to think that we can apply each approach neatly by itself (which could be feasible sometimes), in reality, this is not often the case. Also, the order in which the approaches are chronologically placed *does not* mean that the higher up the approach, the more important it is. This was done merely for the purpose of smoothness and fluidity.

Finally, I would be misleading you if I presented the points briefly. I think there are many   books available on the market claiming to teach the ability to manipulate others, but many are built on speculation and look at the subject from a single angle, whereas this handbook, attempts to incorporate solid, factual methods and information taken from diverse disciplines. Therefore, I urge you to keep these points in mind once you start reading the approaches or steps of the manipulation plan.

1. Start with a Plan (Main Strategy)

"If you don't know where you are going,
how can you expect to get there?"
-Basil S. Walsh

"Our goals can only be reached through a vehicle of a plan,
in which we must fervently believe, and upon which we
must vigorously act. There is no other route to success."
-Stephen A. Brennan

"By failing to prepare, you are preparing to fail."
-Benjamin Franklin

"A man who does not plan long ahead
will find trouble at his door."
-Confucius

"The war is not won at the battlefield, but
in the way you prepare for it."
-Mao

Most of us dread the words *strategy* and *tactics* because they tend to confer feelings of anxiety and confusion. I am not a strategist and this book is not meant to be about strategy in its technical term. You also won't need to have studied or read about strategy, either.

Basically, a *strategy* is a plan of action designed to achieve a particular goal. So for the purposes of this book, **strategy = plan**. Nothing can be achieved in the heat of the moment. Planning is the most crucial part in achieving your goals. Whether you are up against an organisation, a group or an individual, be sure that you have the plan ready and in place.

Tactic is the ability to make decisions on the fly. If strategy is the overall plan, the ability to manoeuvre during the battle is the tactic. So, for us, **tactic = ability to manoeuvre**. A good strategy needs room for tactical flexibility in order to succeed.

One of the most famous advocates for clear planning was Field Marshal Bernard Montgomery, who was a key figure in winning World War II. Montgomery's hallmark as a strategist was a detailed analysis of his enemy and the development of a clear vision as to how that enemy was to be fought and defeated. Two words sum up the approach of the British commander: *clarity* and *organisation*. These were put into practice through careful preparation of what he termed a "master plan," to which all subsequent effort was to be subordinated. The "master plan" embodied the vision, and the strategic and tactical approaches that would be used to achieve it.

Let us now state the components of our own "master plan," which we will term a "manipulation plan." We will start by giving the main headings and then elaborate on each one, individually. Do not panic if you find the terms too technical or if you feel that the elaboration is not clear. We will touch on most of the points of the planning process in more detail in the subsequent sections.

A. Have a simple mission, vision and values
B. Know your enemy's resources by gathering information
C. Analyse the environment
D. Notate the ways to achieve your goals and objectives
E. Anticipate every possibility and allow room to manoeuvre (tactics)
F. Review of the plan

A. Have a simple mission, vision and values:

Take your time. There is no such thing as wasting time in coming up with a plan. Time is your ally if you use it wisely and constructively. In terms of targeting an individual for the sake of manipulation, breaking down or controlling, your initial aim is stating your **mission**. That means it is your main objective now (i.e. the present target). The mission statement should be simple, brief and direct to the point. For instance "control individual A," "breakdown individual A" or "destroy the career of individual A." The mission should be specific as illustrated by the above examples. It should be your motto and as easy to remember as your name.

Once a mission is made (i.e. a target is chosen), the next step is to determine your **vision**. This is a precise, well-crafted set of words announcing where you're heading, or painting a picture of what you want to become. It is a compass showing where and in which direction you're moving. A vision statement not only points the way to the future, but makes you want to get up and go there. Examples include, "to be promoted in X time," "have my philosophy directing company X in X time," and "to get rid of such-and-such person within X time."

A **value** statement in this case is directly related to your ethics and morality and what you are willing to do ethically to achieve your mission. This point was covered in the section about morality and ethics. The crucial point is for you to be comfortable ethically regarding what you're doing and going to do. This is entirely your decision to make and as we said previously, you are the one who "draws the line."

B. Know your enemy's resources by gathering information:

To be able to draw the goals and objectives for achieving your mission (target), good information gathering is crucial. The more information you obtain, the better the outcome and the easier your task will be.

Be a good researcher or detective. Try to find all available bit of information and every detail about your subject. *Nothing is too trivial*: as Julius Caesar said, "In war important events result from trivial causes."

Obtain information directly or indirectly, but be careful not to draw attention to yourself. Information about your target can be found in factual documents, in casual conversations directly with the target or a person known to the target. Information, in terms of type, could be any data, such as personal, factual information, knowledge about the target's social and professional networks, work and family environments plus much more.

Personal information gives you an indication of the state of mind, emotional state and the personality of your target. These things are *vital* because they are your *key* to a triumphant manipulation. Things like the temperament of the person, their prevailing mood, their coping strategies under stress, their family situation, sensitive personal information and what types of friends they have, are crucial. Knowledge of your opponent's characteristic strengths and weaknesses, are also extremely useful.

You win debates and battles by using emotional factors; unlike what many people think, "intellectual" argument will not work, unless it induces an emotional reaction. In your case your goal is to provoke *negative emotions* in your target, such as: fear, anger, sadness and anxiety. Once your goal is achieved, no matter how *intelligent* your enemy is, they become easy prey for any kind of manipulation. *In a nutshell:* aim to target emotions not cognitions (i.e. thinking or intellect).

C. Analyse the environment:

As we said previously, a good plan involves good research prior to entering a conflict. Scan your environment. Look at every factor in the surrounding area. It is not enough just to gather information about your opponent, as mentioned in the previous section. You need to look 360 degrees around them. This should cover all the major aspects of the situation that surround you and your target. Imagine the information about the environment as a large circle and the information regarding your opponent as a smaller circle within it.

This includes the nature of the conflict, the directions your opponent may head to, and any person or factor involved directly or indirectly in the surrounding vicinity of the battlefield. You should look at each of these areas in detail and come up with a list of both the opportunities that the environment offers and the threats that you're facing. Based on your observations, you can then decide when and where to strike. Pay special attention to how your environment and opponents operate and you are bound to find predictable ways in which your target behaves, or routines that your opponent carries out almost religiously, especially because the narcissist tend to be rigid and inflexible

D. Notate the ways to achieve your goals and objectives:

Goals are the broad results that you're committed to achieving. **Objectives** are the steps that you need to take to reach your goals. The right goals make you more effective (i.e. doing things right) while the right objectives make you more efficient (i.e. doing the right thing).

Focus on your goals and elaborate on your objectives. Many collapsed projects and stories of failure are caused by poor planning. A plan which was created in the heat of the moment with brief objectives; has insufficient information-gathering, or had underestimated the mechanism by which to achieve the desired goals, has small likelihood of success. Something which may appear simple on paper is completely different in real life. Therefore, do not underestimate your goals because they *appear simple* to achieve.

E. Anticipate every possibility and allow room to manoeuvre (tactics):

Anticipate the likely obstacles in detail; draw a list even for things that are very unlikely to go wrong. Surprise is a bad thing in the middle of an operation; it rattles you and could undo whatever you have achieved. Do not panic, and be a good tactician, with enough flexibility to manoeuvre, if faced with unpredictability.

One could manage few unpredictable factors along the way discretely, but as the number increases, the likelihood of making a mistake increases. Anticipating as many factors as possible along the way will make your plan run smoothly, effortlessly and also will not attract the attention of others.

F. Review the plan:

Once the plan is ready, and if it is a solid one, try to stick to it. However, no matter how good you are at planning and how much anticipation and information there is, prepare to be flexible and allow room to manoeuvre. But ideally do not skew widely from your plan and if you have to veer from it, try to find a proper solution which brings you back on track to the original plan.

In summary, planning is the first step to conquering your opponent. Take your time, invest effort and only start waging war once you are satisfied with your plan. Do not make the common error of planning as you go, because the probability of failure is higher as the number of unpredictable variables you are likely to encounter, increases. If these are not considered in your plan, they will be impossible to manage and may give the game away.

2. Flourish a Fight and Thrive on Adversity

"Three cheers for war in general."

-*Benito Mussolini*

"War is delightful to those who have not experienced it."
-*Desiderius Erasmus*

"Adversity is a fact of life. It can't be controlled.
What we can control is how we react to it."
-Anonymous source

"Adversities do not make a man frail. They
show what sort of man he is."
-*Thomas Kempis*

Never start a war if you are not ready emotionally, have fear or foresee failure. Do not underestimate the power of negative thinking. If your mind is negative, it is almost a sure recipe for failure. This is a scientific fact and in human clinical psychology it is the main reason behind depression, anxiety, low self-esteem and other pessimistic outcomes.

Motivate yourself by flourishing when up against a challenge. We, as human beings, grow wiser by experiencing adversity in different situations because it makes us more resilient. If we stay in one place, avoid taking risks and follow a hazard-free routine, then our character and personality will be stunted in term of personal growth.

Even children need to be exposed to a limited amount of stress during childhood in order to develop a stronger personality. A child who is shielded by their parents from any kind of adversity is likely to develop a weak, anxious personality.

If you consider war as adversity (i.e. trouble or misfortune), you ought to look at it, instead, as a character builder. There is no better example than these lesser known facts about Abraham Lincoln. He failed in business a couple of times when he was a young man. He had a very shaky marriage and experienced some serious health problems with his children. Lincoln went into politics and actually lost *nine* elections. However, all the time his many adversities were building strength, courage and character within him.

Of course, as we all know, Abraham Lincoln went on to eventually be elected as President of The United States of America; and was one of the greatest presidents, pursuing bold legislation which resulted in the abolition of slavery.

When it comes to the game and the art of manipulation, look forward to the fact that if you have a clear focus, a sound plan and clear targets in mind, you will derive great pleasure and reward upon achieving your goals – and there is no greater joy than the joy of victory! The battle you're engaged in could be a welcome challenge and an opportunity to overcome adversities, thus building you up into a stronger, tougher disposition. As I say throughout this handbook, war is a game and games ought to be fun and interesting. Adapting this kind of perspective will assist you to relax and approach the challenge with an aura of serenity.

In summary, do not engage in war if you're full of negative thinking or doubt. Welcome and flourish the fight. Think of it as a dare, a tactical game or an experience for personal growth and you will be starting on the road to victory.

3. Do Not "Hit with all your Might." Be Calm as Time is Your Ally

---

"The direct use of force is such a poor solution
to any problem. It is generally employed only
by small children and large nations."

-David Friedman

Eliminate the phrases "sense of urgency" and "no time to waste" from your strategic vocabulary. Be calm. "Hit with all your might," does not work in the manipulation war. In ancient eras where the pace of life moved slowly, time and speed were extremely important in wars, and that's why most ancient strategists advocate acting quickly and with a sense of urgency.

Paradoxically, in the present day when the pace of life is so fast and people are racing against each other, and with the technological advances of today, taking your time is the rule. Hurrying places a great deal of pressure on you, which could cause you to make mistakes or expose yourself to the enemy.

Times have changed. Nowadays, people are much more sophisticated than any time in history. Most dispute involving manipulation – whether in politics or in business – are played like a game of chess. Make a move without anticipating the consequences and you'll end up having to play catch-up and acting defensively by handing over the control to your opponent.

Still, many military leaders advocate the use of direct and full force. In recent eras, the use of full force has seldom resulted in a satisfactory outcome, whether in politics, the military or even with businesses. An example from World War II is that of the Nazi General Rommel, "the Desert Fox." His eagerness to drive for Egypt, when the necessary logistical support was lacking, meant that these drives ultimately failed with great losses. Rommel perceived "unique opportunities" in capturing Egypt and perhaps the Middle East. His eagerness blinded his judgment. This miscalculated keenness had a huge impact on the subsequent course of the war.

Some may argue that many wars are won by direct force – one recent example being The Bosnian War. However, if you examine the war closely, you will discover that was not the case. In Bosnia, after all these years, a fragile peace is still maintained by a constant military watchdog, in this case NATO forces. Think about the huge cost and amount of time that has been wasted.

The initial euphoria felt by the U.S. regarding the Iraq war after George W. Bush declared that the United States had won the conflict, proved premature and I don't need to mention what has happened since; the same also could be said about Afghanistan or Somalia. In Afghanistan, the fundamentalist Taliban have regrouped and currently constitute a creditable threat to the world in terms of terrorism.

Somalia on the other hand, is currently a *rough country* and has the potential to become the new centre for terrorism and criminal activities, offering safe haven for individuals carrying out these actions.

Although it may be a simple analysis, all three countries share somewhat similar history, in terms of U.S policy and action. The three countries were invaded or attacked with the main focus on initial force. The planning, strategic tactics and anticipation of the long run consequences were extremely poor. They were even bordering *naivety* and *immaturity*. In all three countries strategies of "hit with all your might" were adapted, with short term gain, but long-term disasters.

From the business world, one could argue that the current *global economic crisis* is due to both government and corporate unplanned, aggressive approach and short sighted actions. Banks granting high risk loans at very low rates, all at government insistence. Stock markets creating "derivatives" that were not backed by anything of real value. Gamblers playing the market numbers while ignoring the stocks behind the numbers. All this created a bubble that had to break. The end result is a recession, which affected and is affecting millions of peoples' livelihoods. All this, because of mistakes and decisions made by individuals, who are suppose to be *experts*, based on poorly thought, shortsighted and extremely risky tactics.

No longer is quick action a wise step in any organisation in terms of combat. Fundamentally, this quick action tactic is flawed. Granted, sometimes it may payoff, especially in the short term, but that is mostly because of luck rather than proper decision-making.

In cases of individuals or an organisation, we could apply the same general rule and that is, "do not rush and only strike once you are fully prepared." It is true that time is a factor but there are many *other* variables which are also important. Such as available resources, preparation, anticipation, options and many other variables depending on the situation; a proper action plan should be inclusive of all these aspects. Once a balanced and a clear picture of the situation has been planned and is starting to emerge, then one can start employing their strategies calmly and with a clear head.

Calmness is a quality of great leaders. In situations where everyone loses their common sense and acts in the heat of the moment, true leaders emerge and in a perplexed, confused crowd, it is easy for a calm, collected person to take control. Everyone has lost focus; they have a tunnel vision and can only see one outcome. The leader, on the other hand, has the advantage of seeing the full picture. Amongst the chaos around them, they can navigate without difficulty, because they have a clear road map at their disposal.

If we consider the scenario of a personal war, in the context of the manipulation of a devious individual, the tactic of calm actions is another way for you to win the battle. You can use the chaos to your advantage, if it is there. If your enemy hits hard with full and quick force, know for certain that you can easily counteract their action because it is bound to be full of gaps waiting to be exploited.

To take this tactic a step further, to your benefit, you could create an illusion of chaos and urgency yourself, thereby inducing the opponent into taking a quick action. Once this transpires then you can manipulate the situation according to your terms.

Some may claim that the element of surprise is an advantage, but this argument is outdated. In this era of modern technology and communication, if you are bamboozled by the element of surprise then you have neglected to do your homework, because it means that you have either failed to anticipate the attack or have deployed a wrong tactic. If you go back to the section about good planning and anticipation, you must realize that you have made a major error and have lost the battle by being a poor strategist or tactician.

In my opinion, the element of a surprise strike is an old tactic that should be reserved for the archives of history, especially in the manipulation war. No modern strategist should by defeated by this tactic nor should they employ it, because the outcome is likely to be failure. Even if, initially, it appears as a success, in the long term it will ultimately be proven otherwise.

The best recent example is the tactic employed by U.S. forces invading Iraq with the so-called "shock and awe." The opposite example is The Cold War. Although the latter, lasted for decades, it was a success overall because, not only did a whole government collapse, but even more impressively, an ideology – Communism – was crushed.

In summary, in this modern day and age, taking your time to plan an elaborate manipulation strategy is a must. Do not feel pressured to act quickly because of emotional factors. The more devious or bigger your target, the more time you should devote to your action plan. "Hit with all your might" is an outdated tactic because it is *fundamentally* full of weaknesses that could be exploited by your opponents. Even if quick action appears to have been successful in the short term, it is likely to fail and prove costly in the long term.

4. Learn Not to Worry, Confront your Fears and Replace Unhelpful Beliefs

---

"Worry a little bit every day and in a lifetime you will lose a couple of years. If something is wrong, fix it if you can. But train yourself not to worry.

Worry never fixes anything."
-*Mary Hemingway*

"War, as the saying goes, is full of false alarms."
-*Aristotle*

This section in some ways is related to the previous one (Number three of the strategic steps). However, while the previous section deals mainly with one's attitude prior to starting a battle, this segment of the strategic components is more inclusive, and it involves one's attitude and belief throughout the battle.

Human being's primary negative emotions are: anxiety such as stress, nervousness, fear, etc.; anger such as frustration, resentment, irritation, etc.; and depression such as unhappiness, sadness, grief, fatigue, low-motivation, etc. Like any tool in your armoury, negative emotion manipulation could be used against you or you could employ it in your favour.

An important fact to always remember is that no matter how strong or powerful an emotion is, it is *always* preceded by a thought. The time between thinking and emotion (reaction to thinking) can be a split second. Nevertheless, from a practical point of view, this fact has tremendous implication.

What that means is, the ability to control, or learning to control, your thinking will enable you to control your emotions. This statement is backed by scientific evidence and is considered a robust fact within the field of cognitive neuroscience. Perhaps a lot of you have come across or read a book about things like anger management, building self esteem or winning people over. Many of these modern self-help books out there are based on the fact that thinking leads to emotional reactions. This simple concept is the foundation behind the wave of *new generation* self-help handbooks flooding the market.

Any failure, if analysed from the above standpoint, will have a primary negative emotion as its trigger. Whether you fail a test, an interview, a war or almost any kind of controllable situation, it is these negative emotions that are behind the failure. In fact, in large doses, these negative emotions could lead to clinical depression, anxiety, performance and social phobias and other psychological problems.

It is not the goal of this book to give detailed solutions to overcoming these emotions, but merely to point out to you, to acknowledge their existence, and that there is a solution to counteract them. When you're facing an opponent and expecting the worse, or you find yourself anxious, fearful or having other negative emotions, then you are controlled by them and the likely outcome is that your negative expectation will become true as a self-fulfilling prophecy.

There are many types of self-help books on the market and all kinds of books written by so called "experts" claiming to help tackle the emotional control subject. This book is not interested in what *may* work, but only in what has been proven to work over and over again by thousands of valid and reliable studies. If you are interested, and find that your negative outlook is a major obstacle impacting your life and hindering you from achieving your potential, then my advice is to read about a form of therapy called *Cognitive Therapy.*

The concept of the therapy is simple and, more importantly, makes practical and common sense. There are neither *Oedipus* or *Electra* complexes nor any other Psychoanalytical concepts to be learned. So, please do not be put off by the term "therapy." Examining your own cognition (thinking) is a practical, easy-to-apply way of learning how to teach the mind to take more control over the emotions.

I will merely touch upon the general concept of cognitive examination as a tool for our main purpose of manipulation, and focus on how to use it to achieve beneficial and desired outcomes.

Thinking → Emotion → Action: All you need to know is this simple factual information. The next time you find that a negative emotion is crippling you or taking over, remember this simple concept and no matter how *emotional* you are, you can overcome it by controlling your thinking.

An example of this is when you are in front of your manipulative and cruel boss and you find yourself full of anxiety. This negative emotion will then lead you to behave restlessly and appear submissive. Your body will start displaying signs of the prevailing emotion – in this case anxiety. You will start to look away and avoid eye contact, your heart beating faster, you're sweating, even trembling, and are experiencing other nasty, unpleasant signs – which I am sure we all have experienced during an anxiety provoking situation.

Prior to any anxious emotions, even if it seemed to appear "out of the blue," there was a thought process, which preceded this anxiety. This is what is called negative thinking. By definition it means a distorted fact and something not genuine, no matter how real it may have felt at the time.

Now let us use revisit the same scenario and examine what is likely to have happened, by using our concept: Thinking → Emotion → Action. Before you had the anxious feelings, a negative thought such as: "Oh my God! He is going to humiliate me" or "Here he comes! This always ends up badly," or "I hate this guy! He is such a tyrant!" popped into your mind. Now, it is no wonder, that if these kinds of thoughts are in your mind, you will almost certainly start to feel anxious which will lead to anxious emotion. This then will be followed by nervous behaviour which will in turn reinforces the initial thinking. Soon you become trapped in a vicious cycle of anxiety with all its undesirable consequences. Such as appearing weak, having low self esteem, perceived as an easy to control person. All of which are disastrous if you are involved in a manipulation game.

So what can you do to stop or prevent this? You need to start by capturing the negative thought *during* the situation. Ask yourself "What was going through my mind before I met my boss and had this anxious feeling?" Once you are able to capture the negative thought, then you are almost there; capable to exert control over your emotion, and in the process, dictating how you react and appear in front of others and according to your terms.

Harness the thought process and examine it in more detail. Dissect it and neutralise it. There are many ways to do this and as I said earlier, there are simple books on the market which offer many techniques to guide you to do so. With our nasty boss example, let's assume that the main thinking was, "Here he comes! This always ends up badly." A simple cognitive approach to overcome this thought is for you to write down lists of what are the beneficial advantages and disadvantages of thinking in this negative way. I'll bet you will find the disadvantages list will be much, much longer than the advantages list.

The above may appear like a too easy technique to achieve positive results (too good to be true). The brain is an amazing and adaptable organ. When you have the information dissected and examined, as in the previous example, you will be surprised at the result. As the brain, almost automatically, will make use of the new knowledge and then utilise it to counteract your anxiety. Try this simple technique next time you find yourself having a negative emotion and witness the result for yourself.

Now we go back into how this knowledge could help us achieve our goal. After all, this is not a text book about therapy, but a handbook teaching you how to manipulate or breakdown deceitful, narcissistic and devious individuals at time of war.

Successful leaders and people do not win wars by letting their negative emotions take over. If there is one thing to take away from this book, it is that the route to controlling others is to have the ability to control your emotions. Think with your brain not your heart. If you allow your emotions to take over when you are at war then believe me, you're a goner!

This may sound like a cruel statement but unfortunately it is an actuality. Let your emotions control you and that's fine, but don't expect that you will climb the ladder of success when you are up against manipulative individuals. We live in the real world and it is an unfair one. Good things happen to bad people and bad things happen to good people. If you are against this principle and consider yourself a person who is guided by their emotions, then good for you, but this book is really not meant for you!

In summary, just remember this vital fact: **Thinking ⊠ Emotion ⊠ Action**. This simply means you cannot control your emotion unless you're able to control your thinking. Manipulation is basically based on the principle of letting your thinking control your emotions and letting your opponents emotions control their thinking. If you grasp this principle then you have mastered the main principle tactic of manipulation.

5. Listen More, Talk Less and Never Interrupt

"There are people who, instead of listening to
what is being said to them, are already listening
to what they are going to say themselves."

-Albert Guinon

"When people talk, listen completely.
Most people never listen."

-Ernest Hemingway

"Never interrupt your enemy when he is making a mistake."

-Napoleon Bonaparte

"Silence is the most perfect expression of scorn."

-George Bernard Shaw

We have all come across the situation where you have spoken to a stranger in a social gathering and once the conversation ends we find ourselves thinking "You know what? I liked that guy, there was something about him." Also, there are situations where the opposite is true. The most likely reason is that in the first situation, the likeable person (the charmer) is a good listener and in the second, he is a poor listener or a talker.

We, humans, love to listen to our own voices. During conversations there is a battle raging which has to do with control. In general, consciously or unconsciously, we talk more than we listen. A lot of us assume that we are able to put our point across by dominating the conversion; this becomes more intense if we are *emotional* or *passionate* about what we are talking about.

In a manipulative strategic term, the facts actually are overwhelming regarding the benefits of listening rather than talking. Listening more and talking less, offers several advantages, which are listed below:

- By allowing your opponent to talk, you gain information about them and as we have said throughout, information is powerful ammunition for your weaponry.

- The more a person talks, statistically speaking, the more likely it is that they will make a mistake or a "slip of the tongue." Give encouragement to your opponent to talk and do not interrupt, especially when they are emotional, as the possibility of making mistakes is high. This is because when we are emotional, we monitor our speech less efficiently.

- By listening, you give little away verbally, hence preventing exposing yourself and giving your opponent valuable information which they may potentially use against you.

- Verbal communication only confers around 40% of what you communicate; the rest is done non-verbally (60%). Nonverbal communication is more reliable and "honest" than verbal communication. By decoding the opponent's body language and with the addition of the verbal communication, you can obtain a very accurate reading of what the person is really communicating as opposed to what they are pretending to communicate. As Peter F. Drucker said, "The most important thing in communication is hearing what isn't said."

- By listening, your task is made easier as you are able to observe the body language and gestures and, as Ludwig Wittgenstein puts it, "The human body is the best picture of the human soul." Added to verbal communication, if you *really* listen and look at both verbal and nonverbal communication, you're mathematically able to observe 100% of the other person's communication.

On the other hand, when we talk, our focus and mental energy is placed on verbal communication and we tend to listen to our own voice. Also, we are unable to monitor our non-verbal communication effectively, which can give away what we are *really* communicating (remember the 60% – 40% rule). This means that a person talking – listening to the sound of their own voice – can hardly obtain any information about the listener. Even if we think that we're being very observant during talking, we still end up having gained no more than 20% of the information about the other person. So listen and observe, and you can potentially obtain 100% information about your opponent: or talk and obtain 20%. I know which one I would choose!

- A simple way to make people like you (be a charmer or alluring) is based on boosting their ego by listening. You can leave an immensely favourable impression by doing the following in a first meeting. Listen and reciprocate (i.e. respond actively) by using body gestures which reflects the talker's mood. Such as nodding in agreement when the talker is stating a fact about what he or she want to put across. Smiling when the talker smiles, and frowning when the talker is conveying sad or unpleasant information. All these are called "modelling" in terms of body language.

- To be even more *likeable*, when you're listening, imagine that you are in a conversation with the most interesting human being you will ever meet in your life. Even if it is the opposite and they are the most boring person you have ever met. As we said, human beings love their egos to be boosted and the above is a powerful way to do so.

- In general, when you are conversing, try to listen over 70% of the time and talk less than 30%. Of course that cannot always be the case and it depends on the setting, but it is a fairly good rule to follow if you want to leave a good impression on someone.

- A lot of people who dominate a conversion think that they had the upper hand or that they "dazzled," because the other person was smiling or nodding throughout the conversion. Big mistake. The real impression you leave is generally unfavourable, as you appear authoritarian, selfish and self-absorbed. If you watch someone totally dominating a conversion, hardly letting anyone else talk and with people smiling around them, you will notice that after the dominant person has finished talking, they leave with a big grin on their face. What they did is that they *fooled* themselves into thinking that they were "the life of the party" or the centre of attention or more tragically thinking that they are an eloquent communicator. Wrong on every score!

- There is one final way to leave a favourable impression. It is a tricky one because it depends on the setting and your skill as a communicator, as it can backfire if it goes wrong. In this situation, you again imagine that you're listening to the most interesting person in the universe, and that you have a limited time with them, so you want to know as much about them as possible. By adopting this approach you will again show real interest in the person, boosting their ego, ventilating and allowing them to hold forth, which all leave a good impression about you.

While using this tactic, attempt two things: *The first*, is to ask them personal questions about such things as their family, hobbies or issues they are passionate about, while being very attentive in the process. Again, you are leaving a favourable impression, plus you are obtaining vital information.

The second is to learn to deflect the conversation from being about you; this has to be done delicately. For example, if the person asks you "What do you do?" you can answer briefly "I am a doctor /lawyer, etc." and then turn things around by echoing the question and by asking what it is that they do. This has deflected the topic of conversion from yourself to them. Now press your advantage. Follow up by asking for more details, not in an interrogative way, but in a curious, interested way. It is critical to keep monitoring what and how much you say, and if you notice that you are talking too much, you should interrupt yourself by saying something like, "Enough about me," and then follow it by a non-threatening question preferably of interest to the speaker (even if it is about their stamp collection!).

In summary, a lot of us love to listen to our own voice and assume that others do too. The facts show that listening is an extremely powerful tool to obtain information and give a favourable impression, which all could serve you in your plan to manipulate that person. So when it comes to your enemy, follow the general rule "Shut up and listen!" and take on board Will Rogers's advice, "Never miss a good chance to shut up."

6. Rumours and Gossip

"A rumor without a leg to stand on will
get around some other way."

-John Tudor

"Whoever gossips to you will gossip about you."
-Spanish Proverb

"The only time people dislike gossip is
when you gossip about them."
-Will Rogers

Rumours could be divided, for the sake of simplicity, into *positive* (i.e. good things said about you or others behind the scenes) and *negative*. The fascinating fact is, once *circulated*, negative rumours tend to stay negative and grow stronger and become more distorted than their original start. On the other hand, positive rumours rarely stay that way after "doing the round" and in the process transform into negative ones!

Understanding this fact can be a powerful weapon in your arsenal, because if you are aware of the above process of rumour formation, it makes it an ideal low risk tactic. Meaning that if you use it correctly it can cause maximum damage, and if it is used against you and you're aware of the above fact, it should have little impact on you because you know that the rumours are unreliable and you cannot read too much into them.

That does not mean you should ignore them; on the contrary, you could counter them or use them as a source of information, because no matter how distorted they are, once they reach your attention, there is almost always a grain of truth in them. More importantly, you should attempt to locate the source of the initial rumours, because that person is a potential enemy that you may know or you may have neglected. If the latter is the case, then you need to counter act the source by fighting back using your manipulation tactics.

As well as the above uses of rumours, mentally, they require little effort and time. Because once you start the ball rolling, a rumour will take on a life of its own and you can just sit back and watch it grow as the rest of the work will be done by others, unlike most tactics where you need to do the majority of the work.

If you are able to remain calm about negative rumours targeted towards you, and realise the fact they will most likely trigger an emotional response, then you have obtained a tactical advantage.

An excellent example from ancient history of using rumours tactics concern The Mongols, led by Genghis Khan. During their invasions, The Mongols made sure that before conquering the next city or town, that rumour about their cruelty (e.g. rivers of blood, killing pregnant women) and invincibility (e.g. that Mongols are immortals) had reached the enemy. In fact, many cities surrendered without even a fight because of the fears created by these terrifying rumours. The same could be said about Attila the Hun when he conquered Europe.

Many "Holy Wars" also employed these tactics, with rumours reaching the enemy of armies of "angels sent by God" to fight alongside their opponents (e.g. The Crusade). The Nazis also engaged this tactic when they started to invade Europe, with rumours of "superhuman, unbeatable soldiers" reaching the opponents and creating fear and chaos.

In modern times, we all know the powerful effect the media has in spreading rumours, and I would urge you to look up the late, great actor Orson Welles and his use of the radio as a tool in the prank to publicise his adaptation of H.G. Wells' novel, *War of the Worlds*, when he was able to create mass hysteria in the public by convincing them that Martians actually had invaded Earth!

Rumours can be spread directly or indirectly. In our era, the indirect route is preferable as it offers you anonymity. If you are targeting an individual enemy, a simple way to start a rumour is to scan your environment and find a source of *dispersion*: a person who you know cannot keep their mouth shut. Once a rumour starts, just sit back and see how quickly it spreads and how powerful its impact on the enemy is.

As we also mentioned, we are in a different era now, and the use of technology such as e-mails – just make sure that you don't send an email from your own account! – could be employed. This emphasises the point that you have to modernise and use every means at your disposal in order to achieve your objectives. Again, the Mongols are an excellent example, as they used everything and anything at their disposal, which was one of their main strengths at the time.

A fascinating example of how simple this tactic is to use, was told to me by a friend working in a large firm, who targeted a manipulative opponent by simply writing a negative rumour about that person containing personal information (to induce a negative emotion) on a piece of paper and left it lying on the staff coffee room. Within a few days, almost every person in the firm was gossiping about that person, which caused him to reach breaking point.

In summary, do not underestimate the power of rumours and gossip. Understand their formation, advantages and disadvantages. They are a simple, low risk and low effort tactic which, if used appropriately, could cause huge damage to your manipulative opponent.

7. Doubt

"Our doubts are traitors, and make us lose the good we oft might win by fearing to attempt."

-William Shakespeare

"Doubt whom you will, but never yourself."

-Christine Bovee

Behind the loss of any battle, doubt is one of the first stages of defeat. Your task is twofold regarding this recipe for loss. *The first* is to make sure that it never enters your *psyche* (mind). *The second* is to use it against your potential enemy as one step toward victory.

To achieve your *first objective*, it is not enough just to *assume* that you're strong enough about your capabilities, making you immune to doubt. Again, as we have mentioned before, doubt originates from emotions. So to prevent an element of doubt from entering your mind, there are many preventative steps you can take which, in one way or another, we have already touched upon in our discussion. However, for the sake of focus, I shall list the main steps you can take to prevent or counteract this negative emotion:

- Let your brain guide your heart, i.e. intellect determine emotion (or what I call intelligent emotions as opposed to emotional intelligence).

- Anticipation and good planning will reduce the risk of doubt.

- Monitor yourself, and if there is even the faintest suggestion that doubt is entering your mind, avoid denial and face it. Rationalise your thought and remember that thinking determines emotions, so dissect your thinking and reflect deeply, until you reach the source of this doubt and eliminate it by removing the negative thinking behind it. Do not wait for doubt to germinate, and consider eradicating it a priority if you notice the first signs, or even a faint hint of this defeatist attitude developing.

- Never ever start a war or confrontation if you have a doubt in your mind. Deal with your doubt first. That will automatically build your confidence and you will be on the right track and at the proper place to start. Remember that it is quite alright to wait and not rush into battle until *almost* all circumstances are in your favour and a thorough plan and strategy are in place.

If you try, and fail, to eliminate doubt during the heat of the battle, it is okay to retreat. After all, one of the main goals of this book is discretion, so if you are invisible and unnoticed, there is no harm in retreating; in fact, you could consider your retreat as a relaxing pause and a positive step, allowing you to rethink, regroup and then hopefully restart with vigour and determination.

The *second objective* is to use doubt for your benefit. Hopefully, by now, the above discussion has equipped you with the knowledge of the usefulness of doubt as a weapon. It is a foundation shaker and in battle, doubt is a crucial step in breaking the enemy's infrastructure and one of the initial steps and tactics along the road to victory.

No matter how strong your opponents appear, no human being is immune to doubt. It is within our evolutionary build and keeping this fact in mind is important. Planting the seed of doubt is your goal. This could be done using many tactics and approaches such as rumours, deception, triggering negative emotions and many tactics we will touch upon later, or have touched upon previously. The objective is simple: plant the seed of doubt and, with the addition of other tactics, you will soon see your enemy crumble as they lose focus and become erratic, unsure and disorganised.

Doubts shake foundations, and therefore destroy even the strongest enemies and the most well thought out and well-planned strategies. It is a tactic often underestimated and underused; or, if used, it is considered of a secondary importance. If that is the case with your opponent, then it is a huge advantage for you and a sure way, not only to aid you in winning, but also to help shorten the length of the battle because you will be targeting the infrastructure and counteracting the enemy's strategy at its initial stage.

Here is an *indirect approach* example, which works well in an organisational setting (e.g. a company, a factory or even a college). If you want to make your opponent doubt what you're thinking, a simple tactic is to use a vague e-mail, written correspondence or a phone call with an emotionless tone (the fancy term for this is "prosody") with the aim of making your opponent uncertain about the source's intentions. We human beings cannot cope with anticipating the unknown for a long period. This type of doubt tactic creates this "anticipatory anxiety," which is very consuming physically and mentally. Also, it is well known to lead to "mental breakdown" if it lasts for a long period of time.

If, on the other hand, you're sure of what you want, then face to face (*direct approach*) is the way to go and it has the biggest impact, if used properly. Let us imagine a scenario where you think an opponent is gossiping or undermining you behind your back. You could simply create doubt by implying that you have spoken to a close colleague of your manipulative opponent and leave it at that. This, in turn, whether true or false, would make them think about what has been said, who to trust or, even better it may generate a conflict between your opponent and their friend, especially if you did not actually speak to their friend in the first place! Remember that trust is an issue with a person with narcissistic, manipulative characteristics.

In summary, when you start waging a manipulation war, try to prevent doubt from entering your mind. Moreover, generate doubt in your manipulative enemy sooner rather than later, as it will shake their confidence, make them erratic, suspicious and easy to destroy early on, saving you time and effort. Do not underestimate this powerful tactic, because I assure you that it is extremely effective, in most settings, against a manipulative individual.

8. Select your Targets Carefully and One at A Time

"An army of sheep led by a lion would defeat an army of lions led by a sheep."

-Arab Proverb

As we mentioned earlier, the first step in any manipulation plan is the mission, where you choose the target. We have also mentioned that this handbook could be used primarily against individuals and secondarily against groups or even large organisations. In this section I will attempt to elaborate on this point as it is important in your initial planning.

Once you have thoroughly scanned and identified your target (your mission), it is important that you focus on this target and devise your plan according to the information you were able to gather about this individual. This target does not necessarily have to be the highest in term of status in an organisation.

Often the case is that the source of a problem is a person working in the shadows, or working for what *appears* to be your source of difficulties (e.g. your boss). It is important tactically that you target the mastermind or the person pulling the strings (e.g. an adviser to your boss).

Do not be deceived into automatically thinking that your boss (for example) is the source of the difficulties, even if the problem *appears* to originate from them (e.g. a warning letter signed by your boss). It may well be that another person close to them is behind this. Here is where taking your time and gathering accurate information is the key to a successful campaign.

It would be futile to manipulate the boss in the above scenario. You need to target the mastermind who is usually a manipulator themselves and are successful in controlling the boss. This person should be your primary target.

If you're working in a setting with more than one target, then you have two priorities. Firstly, try to establish *who* the biggest source of your problem is. Secondly, *target* and focus on that person and avoid the temptation to battle more than one target at a time. Each person is different and will require a different manipulation plan. Once you achieve your desired goal by manipulating the main person by eliminating, controlling or neutralising them, you move to the next one in the list and so on.

Sometimes, with an organisation, the case is that even if it appears that there are many potential targets, once you eliminate this one individual (i.e. the mastermind), the rest will collapse naturally like a house of cards. If that is the case, then it is excellent for you, as you do not need to move further by targeting other people.

If, however, that is not the case, then you need to shift your attack to the next person in the strategic list. Be aware that this new target will require a different strategy and set of tactics to break them down. Don't make the mistake of assuming that a successful plan that served you well in manipulating the first person, would work with the second target on your list. This is rarely the case, as each person will have their own unique constitution with different information, agenda, mind-set and characteristics, requiring you to devise a new plan specifically tailored for that particular manipulator.

Ideally, you should have anticipated this from the start, but if you did not, don't worry. Start the process from the beginning and, as we have often pointed out, take your time and gather as much sensitive information as possible before you attack. Do not let the euphoria of your first success blind you or deceive you into acting quickly and with complacency.

Occasionally, after consolidating your plan, you may be lucky enough to discover that two of your targets are fighting against each other, or have fundamentally different agendas (narcissistic individuals often do). This is an excellent opportunity for you, as all you have to do is use a few tactics (e.g., rumours, deception) to make them battle each other. Meanwhile, you're in the background watching, observing the ensuing clash and gathering information about the tactics they are using, which may aid you in doing battle with whoever emerges as the victor!

If you adopt the above strategy, you can target individuals, groups or even an organisation. Just remember to be patient and that planning is the key. An essential point which this book aims for is discretion, stealth and being invisible while you're applying your strategy and tactics. This point will be mentioned later under a separate heading, but I hope it is obvious to you from the above example why this point is critical in modern manipulation warfare.

In summary, in the process of planning, especially in today's modern setting, you are likely to encounter more than one enemy. You have to take your time, gather information and prioritise who to target first. Do not assume that a person with a higher status or rank is always the mastermind, as there maybe another person of a lower rank who is pulling the strings and maybe even manipulating that person. So focus your energy and effort in planning to hit the primary target and then, if needed, move on to the next in your list by approaching them with a new plan and a fresh start.

9. Underestimation

"The dumber people think you are,

the more surprised they're going to be when you kill them."
-*William Clayton*

"There's no underestimation but we'll use this strength to our

advantage."
-*Ifereimi Tawake*

Underestimation, as a weapon which could be used by or against an opponent, is often a tactic which is rarely incorporated in ancient and even modern planning. Too often, we tend to concentrate all our effort and energy on enemies we consider formidable, while underestimating others whose role in our problems is less obvious. We have this tunnel vision, whereby we use all our energy and resources to fight the formidable, clear and visible challenger.

Rarely do we scan the environment to look for emerging potential foes, and worse still, if there is one we deem unthreatening because of their lower status or influence, we tend to ignore them, believing that the current and present danger is the priority.

Underestimation, throughout history has destroyed civilizations, companies, organisations and individuals. We seem to ignore this repeated and recurrent historical theme. We devote little if any effort to keep an eye on what we consider unequal to us in term of power or authority.

I am not asking you to devote a huge amount of time and planning on every small or emerging potential rival, but just to consider them in your plan by constantly monitoring and scanning your environment, which should be a part of your strategy.

Nothing remains the same and power shifts regularly with time. Ignore the above at your own peril, because if you do, you could be hit by an unexpected opponent and by then it will be too late to do something about it, because you have not prepared for such an attack. You will not know any information about them, their strengths and weaknesses, their methods and tactics, and all that will result in your demise. As Aristotle said, "No notice is taken of a little evil, but when it increases it strikes the eye."

A lesson from history on underestimation comes from the American Revolution against the British. One of the greater advantages that the Americans held was that the British underestimated them. Even before the war began, an anonymous British officer bragged that the Americans could be beaten by an experienced sheep herder. This remark clearly backfired and we all know what happened next.

Another example is the rise of the Islamic empire that conquered Asia, Northern Africa and part of Europe. The Muslims at that time were considered Bedouins, naive, primitive and inferior to their enemy. This underestimation won them many wars and resulted in the spread of Islam in a remarkably short time. The same could be said about the Mongols.

In the modern day and age, specifically in the world of business, the car industry offers a poignant example. In the 1970s and early 1980s and prior to that, the U.S. was considered the pioneer of the industry. At the same time, the Japanese car industry started and built its foundation on learning from the Americans and attempting to improve by modernising and using customer-centred concepts such as family-oriented designs, economical value for money, reliability and most importantly, utilising the philosophy of improvement as an endless process (now a basic concept in modern quality teaching).

Meanwhile the U.S. became complacent and didn't anticipate the changing attitudes and environment in the world. They not only underestimated the Japanese and didn't even consider them a formidable challenge, but, worse still underestimated the customers' changing attitudes.

Nowadays, the most successful car company in the world is Toyota. While the American car industry is crumbling and most of the old giants of the industry are bankrupt or on the verge of it, with their futures looking bleak.

On the other hand, make it part of your tactics to make your enemies underestimate you. This is especially important in the initial stage and when you are the "new kid on the block." This will keep you off others' radar and allow you to assess the situation and have plenty of time to get to know the surrounding dynamics and environment, making it easier for you to draw up a proper manipulation plan.

Again, this tactic is often underused as we tend to draw attention to ourselves whenever we join a new setting. This is very common, as our enthusiasm and the desire to "make a good impression" seem to be ingrained in us. In the war of manipulation, this is a major mistake, because paradoxically the more impressive you appear initially, the more likely it is that you will have enemies and obstacles in the future, as well as making it hard for yourself to scan and plan unnoticed. So sometimes, it is okay to play dumb, especially if you are new and in a large setting.

In summary, underestimation like most of the approaches we have mentioned, is something you could use to your advantage as it enables you to work your way unnoticed, allowing you to attain your goals unchallenged. Also, it could teach you a lesson about keeping an eye on any future possible opponent even if they are of lesser status or capabilities. Added to that, you must learn not to be complacent and be open to the idea of monitoring and learning from every opponent, no matter how little and "insignificant" they may appear. Finally, sometimes it is an excellent tactic to make others underestimate you, as it allow you to manipulate undetected.

10. Provoking Emotions in an Opponent is A Primary Target

"There is perhaps no psychological skill more fundamental than resisting impulse. It is the root of all emotional self-control, since all emotions, by their very nature,

led to one or another impulse to act."
-Daniel Goleman

"Anger dwells only in the bosom of fools."
-Albert Einstein

"He who angers you conquers you."
-Elizabeth Kenny

This is perhaps the most important strategic component of all in the manipulation game. It is the cornerstone for an effective manipulation plan. Now you have to forgive me if I am repeating a previous point, but because of how *crucial* this part is in our manipulation game, I definitely think (notice I used the word *think* and not *feel!*) it is worth the reemphasis and elaboration.

I would also like you to consider two points throughout the next discussion. The *first* one is to understand the importance of emotions in manipulation (i.e. that it makes sense to you), and the *second* is the process of how to use this knowledge (i.e. that it is practical).

When we are in a situation of extreme adversity, the majority of us tend to let our emotions dictate our actions. That needn't be the case. It is because of this that we could be manipulated, tricked, stressed and depressed plus all sort of other unpleasant things.

Remember that thinking always *precedes* emotions and that is a scientific fact, as has been shown by brain imaging, that the thinking centres becomes activated before the emotional centres (thinking ⊠ emotions). This fact has a huge practical application and implication. So, although it may appear to you that, for example, feeling angry, sad, frightened came out of the blue, that is definitely not the case because a thought occurred before this and actually led to these unpleasant emotions. I realise that I have mentioned this in an earlier section, but I am repeating it here because it is the basis for our current tactic.

Now, some of you may get annoyed because I am about to also go back and talk again about those *bad*/devious/malicious individuals, those with "Narcissistic Personality" characteristics, but after all, isn't it the goal of this book to manipulate and breakdown these people? So a little bit more understanding of the mind-set of these people won't do any harm and I promise to look at it from a different angle than I did previously!

Although it is normal and healthy to take a positive attitude toward oneself, narcissistic persons exhibit an inflated view of self as special and superior. Rather than strong self-confidence, however, narcissism reflects self-preoccupation. The narcissist is very active and competitive in seeking status, as outward signs of status are used as the measure of personal worth. When others fail to validate the special status of the narcissistic person, he or she is apt to view this as intolerable mistreatment and become angry, defensive and depressed. Narcissistic individuals take pride in their social standing, yet show some startling lack in adhering to norms and expectations of social reciprocity (i.e. give and take).

Self-centred and inattentive to the feelings of others, the narcissist can turn a friendly exchange into an irritating display of self-preoccupation. A deceptively warm demeanour may be marred by arrogant outbursts, heartless remarks or insensitive actions. Attention to the needs and feelings of others is lacking, whether in simple matters such as recognising the contributions of others, or in respecting deeply meaningful emotions. They may begrudge the successes of others and jealously judge or discredit those they view as encroaching competitors. The narcissist can also be masterful in twisting confrontations toward attributing blame and fault to other people.

That's enough about those people's characteristics. Now we move into understanding how to use this information to overcome these unpleasant individuals. Especially, while reading the above section many of you may have met or thought back of one or two people, at least, who fit the description of a narcissistic person (a manipulator). Even if you yourself are a narcissist, the funny thing is that because of your mind-set (denial, self importance) you are unlikely to realise that you are one. Also you will have some people in mind – but because of rigidity and socially maladaptive characteristics – in your case they won't be one or two, but tens or even hundreds of people!

The majority of individuals when they attempt to manipulate, make the fundamental mistake of thinking about the person from *their* point of view. In a way this is a normal human reaction, we see the world through our own eyes. We tend to look at others and assume that they have our feelings and our emotions. We do that automatically and often unconsciously.

You need to change this perception if you are to play the manipulation game efficiently. Try to enter the manipulative person's mind, think how they think, and feel what they feel. The only way to do that is by knowing about the person. The more you know, the better you will become at this.

Knowledge of an emotional and sensitive nature, knowing what triggers an emotional reaction in them, makes it easier to have a similar mind-set to the manipulator. Once you think you have enough information then you can predict what that person would do and how they will react. This allows you to start manipulating them, as you will be able to make them tick and induce emotions with your actions (directly or indirectly) and in your own terms.

Everyone is bound to have planted triggers which, if activated or switched on, will cause an emotional reaction. The deeper and more emotion-inducing the concern one has, the more extreme the reaction. Your aim is to discover in the person you're attempting to manipulate, the things that makes them exhibit these extreme emotions such as crying, acting like a child, becoming insecure and other immature emotions which break the personality and shatter it.

Earlier, I mentioned the fact that it is easier to breakdown narcissistic (*bad*) individuals compared to normal, psychologically "healthy," *good* people. Generalisation here is of some value and could act as a guide to discovering the trigger in those manipulative persons. Themes to do with control, success, superiority, self-importance or power are most likely what you're looking for. This kind of predictability is of immensely valuable significance.

From your point of view, take each theme we mentioned and, in an indirect way, try to undermine it in those people. You will soon touch on the ones which cause the most extreme emotions such as an anger outburst, confusion, stress or a change in their usual personality and demeanour.

Let us assume that power is the trigger. What you could do is take steps to undermine this by actions or comments which make them feel powerless. For example, in an organisational setting, by spreading comments of how another person has more say, *power*, than the narcissist (manipulator), or trivialising their power over others – which could all be done indirectly.

Now that you know the triggers, "keep schtum" and do not rush into bombarding them with actions inducing the extreme reaction. You have to play it cool. Be subtle, use stealth and use this knowledge slowly in a calculative way and allow a gap in time in inducing the reaction.

You have to be aware that if you hit these individuals full on, then they will be extremely vindictive and their extreme emotion will be followed by an extreme and over the top reaction. Also, if you do that then you have exposed yourself to their savage attacks which, from their point of view, are justified. You will be right back at square one, in a worse position than the one you started in, because you have used up one of your chief weapons and your enemy will now be on their guard.

Their "revenge" will be relentless, spiteful and carried without remorse. When they attack you and manage to get to you, that will build their self-confidence and with each successful attack, their confidence will be regained and with that, they will start to go back to thinking again, which was your original target you set out to destroy; making their emotion guide their thinking and not the opposite.

So – what to do once you know the trigger in those people? As we said, be calm, remain invisible and plan your action sensibly. Although you may sense victory, do not be deceived by it. The road to manipulate or breakdown these people could take time, as it is a process, a marathon rather than a sprint.

Just imagine that these people who appear so powerful, intelligent and ruthless are hiding behind a thick wall built to protect their fragile ego; a wall that was built brick by brick through deception, ruthlessness and walking over others. It took these narcissists years to assemble and in all the years they hardly sustained any attack, so the wall is solid and rock-hard.

If you attack this wall with all your might, then I can assure you that it will collapse over you and destroy you in the process. What you have to do is take small, effective steps, separated in time. This tactic (small steps at a time) was used by Hannibal in his wars by marching about the enemy flanks to seize cities or supplies in their rear, harassing them with small-war, and rarely venturing into a major battle which might prove a fatal disaster, all with the well-conceived purpose of placing his opponent at a strategic disadvantage.

In the case of the narcissist, imagine yourself walking toward a huge wall or dam without being seen and chipping a little hole in it. You then retreat to a safe distance. Keep repeating this process even if it takes time. After a while, with many chips and cracks in the wall, it will start to crumble naturally, almost like a dam collapsing. The difference is that once this dam breaks down you are at a safe distance, hidden amongst the crowed, gazing in awe at this once mighty wall collapsing and revealing behind it an almost childlike person who has been protected for years by this structure. Once people see them exposed, then game over, mission accomplished.

In summary, the main fact to understand is that our problems stem from our negative emotions. We assume that we are powerless over them, when in fact we could learn to control them. This is the principle of manipulation. Trigger emotions and people lose their common sense and become an easy target to manipulate. Learning to use this tactic requires immense self-discipline, planning, stealth and time. Once you master this, then you will be able to breakdown and manipulate almost anyone especially bad/deceitful/devious people (i.e. the narcissistic, manipulative person).

11. Fear

"No passion so effectually robs the mind of all its powers of acting and reasoning as fear."

-Edmund Burke

"You can discover what your enemy fears most by observing the means he uses to frighten you."

-Eric Hoffer

"To use fear as the friend it is, we must retrain and reprogram ourselves ... We must persistently and convincingly tell ourselves that the fear is here — with its gift of energy and heightened awareness — so we can do our best and learn the most in the new situation."

-Peter McWilliams

Although I could have placed this section as part of the previous section, I elected to devote a separate discussion about this primary negative primary emotion because of its great magnitude. Fear requires a special mention as it is one of the most powerful emotion of all, one which, if you are able to induce it in an individual or even a population, you could easily use to exert control over them.

Major religions and cults use fear – fear of hell, the evil eye, spirits even fear of aliens –as their main tool to control individuals. Other examples of some type of fears, used by modern cultures, are in the workplace (fear of losing job), politics (fear of terrorism/the economy collapsing) and family (fear of punishment by parents). Just to list a few.

We start life as infants, with fear being an inbuilt evolutionary primary instinct. Then throughout our existence, everything revolves around this emotion. When fear takes us over, our common sense is thrown out of the window.

Do not underestimate this powerful emotion; frankly speaking, it is one of the easiest to induce, because once we are born, this instinct is strengthened by our environment such as our family (fear of punishment), school (fear of failure), relationship (fear of abandonment), work (fear of losing our job, making a mistake or competition), fear of authority, fear of wars and the ultimate fear, fear of death.

The result of all these fears was summed up very eloquently by Connie Zweig, "Once you uncover the history of this pattern and trace its roots, you will see that your reaction in the present moment is really a reaction from the past, a shadow character's attempt to protect you from re-experiencing an old emotional wound, which instead sabotages you in the present."

So it is no wonder that politicians, religious leaders and other figures of authority make use of fear, as it is already waiting to be triggered (some might say exploited) to achieve their target and manipulate individual and the masses (think 9/11 and the subsequent "mass hysteria" which made the public "obey" whatever politicians "ordered").

Hannibal, who is often regarded as the greatest military tactician and strategist and one of the most talented commanders in history, was known for his cruelty and used fear as a main weapon against his enemy. He occupied much of Italy for 15 years. For generations, Roman housekeepers would tell their children brutal tales of Hannibal when they misbehaved. In fact, Hannibal became such a figure of terror, that whenever disaster struck, the Roman Senators would exclaim *"Hannibal ante portas"* ("Hannibal is at the Gates!") to express their fear or anxiety.

We could also argue that the modern media is built on a culture of fear because it uses it to grab our attention and increase sales. Look at the front page of any newspaper and I almost guarantee you that the main headline will be a sensational one which induces fear (e.g. flu epidemic, collapse of the economy, a natural disaster, impending war, etc.).

Also, if you just pause, think and examine events in your life which made you irrational, I bet you that the majority will have fear as their underlying trigger. So, use fear on your enemy because it is an effective, fast way to manipulate them. In the list of all the negative emotions, this one in general is the most powerful and the quickest to induce.

In summary, fear is the archetypel of all the negative primary emotions. It has its root in evolution and is ingrained and strengthened in us from infancy by our surrounding environment. Throughout history the use of fear has been a fundamental foundation to achieve whatever result an establishment wanted (religious, commercial, philosophical and so on and so forth). Use this emotion against your opponents through the many strategic guidelines mentioned in the handbook (e.g. rumours, deception) and you are bound to achieve your goal. This emotion if triggered to a maximum level could make anyone lose their rational (intellectual) reasoning and hence be an easy target to manipulate as you wish. On the other hand, realise that fear is part of you, but with this realisation, attempt to control it by remembering the simple fact, that thoughts control emotions and not *vice versa*. So if you find yourself fearful, don't panic, be calm, do not let this emotion take over and try to control it using your mind, not your heart.

12. Anticipation and Predictability

"Never believe any war will be smooth and easy or that anyone who embarks on that strange voyage can measure the tides and hurricanes he will encounter."

-Winston Churchill

"In war we must always leave room for strokes of fortune, and accidents that cannot be foreseen."

-Polybius

"A wise man in times of peace prepares for war."

-Horace

Although we touched very briefly on the subject of anticipation in the Planning section, we promised to elaborate further on its importance both as something to plan, watch out for and as a tool against your opponent.

The most successful companies (e.g. Toyota), strategists (e.g. Kissinger) or war leaders (e.g. Churchill, Alexander the Great) have always placed a great emphasis on, and left room for, the unforeseen. In modern planning a crucial part of a sound plan is to anticipate and reduce risk. This can only be achieved by devoting time and effort to scanning and examining the environment.

Let's go back to the Toyota model as a good example of the above and try to simplify the way the company deals with unpredictability. In Toyota, it is within the company philosophy, which is taught to the entire workforce, that mistakes are bound to happen and unpredictability is likely.

Blaming culture is not the main goal, but learning from mistakes is. If anything unpredictable happens or mistakes are made, the staff member immediately reports it in an organised manner, guided by an established protocol. A procedure of gathering staff and solving the problem *then and there* is done. This ultimately, enables the employee not to repeat the mistake, and to have the means to overcome the problem should it recur in the future. The "new" solution is then incorporated within the company's protocols and every staff member is informed.

Now, the above may sound like a commonsense simple approach. However, in reality most companies and people, once they are faced with a problem, panic, hide it, try to blame others, ignore it (denial) or they use my favourite excuse "We will deal with it later."

As well as the above, Toyota always anticipate the market, leaving room for unpredictable factors (such as economical, social and political factors), look for what the customer wants, and adopt the philosophy that improvement is a never-ending process.

Again, that all sounds simple to replicate and many companies have adopted and imitated the Toyota model, but still many have failed because they ignored the simple fact that it is one thing to put procedures in place and another thing for them to actually work. No matter how good a plan is on paper, if you do not believe in it, trust it and make it part of your thinking then, it is bound to fail. The same applies to you and me. It is one thing *to say* the right thing and another thing *to actually do it*. To do something, you have to believe, otherwise forget it.

Now we go back to the target of reducing risk. One can never eliminate the risk or anticipate all the possibilities However, if you attribute a great importance in your strategy to this crucial aspect, then you will be ready for almost any unforeseen *surprise*. Most plans in modern businesses or militaries fail because of this underestimation of the importance of anticipating difficulties along the way.

You have to understand that the environment is dynamic and so your plan and tactics should be flexible enough to be able to cope with any unanticipated factors. When it comes to manipulating or anticipating the moves of your opponents, you have to expect the unexpected. This is where being a good tactician, able to change your manoeuvre during battle, is crucial.

Alexander the Great is considered by many to be the greatest war leader in history. He never lost a battle in 11 years. Fighting mostly against armies greater in number than his own. Alexander is considered as brilliant tactician. One of his greatest skills was his ability to change the movement of his troops during the heat of battle. Added to that was his ability to install confidence in his troops so that they were not to be fazed by any unpredictability or element of surprise, *during* the heat of battle.

In Alexander's battles in India this discipline was very important. Alexander's men had never seen elephants before they entered those battles. When faced with fighting a man up on top of an elephant, untrained and undisciplined soldiers would most likely have run, but Alexander's well-trained veterans stood their ground. They were confident in their superior's ability to tell them what to do. They didn't run, even when faced with these bigger enemies.

An excellent example of anticipating the unpredictable, taken from the modern day world of business, is that of Johnson & Johnson, a company which is known for its excellent corporate reputation and consistently ranks at the top of the world's most respected and successful companies. In 1982, Extra Strength Tylenol capsules in Chicago-area stores were found to be poisoned with cyanide. Johnson & Johnson's quick but carefully planned response, including a nationwide recall, was widely praised by public relations experts and the media. Unlike many other companies, their action was swift and although the recall cost in terms of monetary value in the short term, the company's reputation was consolidated and its shares increased in value in the long term.

Going back to our goal, the good news is as we said earlier, that "*bad*/manipulative" people, unlike "normal" ones, tend to be more predictable, but that should not and must not be a reason for complacency. For example, even with their *predictability*, there is still an *unpredictable* component. For instance, although you may know that a certain move you make will result in retaliation by the enemy (i.e. a *predictable* response), just what form this retaliation will take, is still difficult to anticipate (e.g. anger, fighting back, retreating, bringing another party into the equation), so that part remains in the realm of the *unpredictable*.

Now, we can look at the unpredictability as a potential weapon in your favour. It is not a contradiction in terms to be predictably unpredictable! What I mean is that in your plan (which is predictable to you), you could make unpredictability an essential component in your attacks (something which is still predictable to you, but not to the enemy). So, with regard to the manipulative opponent make your principle having no principle!

The Duke of Marlborough, considered by many as one of the greatest tacticians in history, deployed this tactic excellently. He was extremely adept. Invariably, he would aim to seize the initiative and be unpredictable in his attacks. For example, he achieved victory in Schellenberg by attacking late in the afternoon. This was an unusual time of day to attack and, having thrown his foe off balance, he delivered the fatal blow.

Vary your tactics and do not adopt the same method again even if it worked. This will make you difficult to detect and also will cause confusion and, better still from your viewpoint, "anticipatory anxiety" in your enemy. The latter is one of the most unpleasant feelings you could ask for and is a sure path to the destruction of the inflicted party.

In summary, when you're drawing up your plan, leave room for possible unpredictable factors, tactics, space to manoeuvre and flexibility to cope with the demand for change if necessary. Be rigid with your plan, and failure will be a likely possibility even if your initial plan was going smoothly (again, the Iraq war is my repeated best example of this). Unpredictable things and mistakes happen no matter how well you're prepared, but do not panic or lose control if something unexpected happens. If that is the case, then deal with it calmly, and consider it valuable information, a lesson and experience for future progress.

13. Use Stealth and be Invisible

"O divine art of subtlety and secrecy! Through you we learn
to be invisible, through you inaudible and hence we can hold
the enemy's fate in our hands."

-Sun Tzu

"No one ever approaches perfection except by stealth, and
unknown to themselves."

-William Hazlitt

"The greatest pleasure I know is to do a good action by stealth
and have it found out by accident."

-Charles Lamb

Churchill once said, "(In war) be discrete." This simple quote, like
many in this handbook, has such an imperative quality which may
seems simple to achieve, but in actual fact requires great discipline and
strength in character.

Perhaps by now you are fed up with listening to me repeating the
significance of being invisible and may wonder why I am placing it
in a separate heading, because I have already touched on it several
times.

Well, my dear reader, it is because it is so vital to our goal. After all, what
we are attempting to do is to breakdown or manipulate our opponent
undetected. In the next part we will talk a bit more in detail about this
point and attempt to expand on its benefit and use in waging an attack
on our target of manipulation.

Let me start by explaining why I said that it requires great discipline. This stems from the fact that most of us, let's faces it, have "a big mouth." As human beings the majority of us find it very hard to keep things to ourselves, especially if it is something that requires great effort and consumes lots of time and energy.

This becomes even harder if what we have attempted is bearing fruits and working. In a way, it is an understandable human nature to want to share our successes with others. Especially, in matters which we deemed too important, required a lot of effort and were successful. We feel this urge to talk about our achievements and our elaborated plans which led us to obtaining our goals.

We also sometimes try to convince ourselves, rightly or wrongly, that it is important for us to "ventilate" or share things with people we are certain are trustworthy and who we think will *never* betray us.

To a certain extent, I agree with these notions. However, as we said throughout, we should let our thinking guide us rather than our emotions. When and if you feel like "ventilating" or "sharing," just remember all the disadvantages that it may potentially bring with it. For the sake of importance, whenever you have the urge to "ventilate" and "share," I want you to consider the following points:

- Being dependent on the person you disclosed to will make you a potential target for manipulation in the future, because a friend today may be an enemy tomorrow.

- Information is a valuable commodity in any war. People are only too willing to sell to the highest bidder, or where they are getting something in exchange (e.g. a promotion, materialistic valuables, favours etc.).

- Remember that your main aim is to be independent, self-reliant and in control of the situation. None of these things will be possible if you "share," "ventilate" or uncover your objectives to another person.

- Always think ahead. Short-sightedness could be your downfall in a long term war or in fighting many wars, which is often the case with manipulation.

- Having the ability to be invisible (not literally of course!) and silent teaches you discipline and builds your character. You want to be a leader and the strength, discipline and ability to remain invisible throughout a long term war is a sign of strong leadership.

- From a psychological point of view, if you operated visibly in front of a person, then even if that person never gives you up, nevertheless, consciously or unconsciously you will always have the seed of insecurity in your mind. This in turn could work to distract you, consume mental energy and, worse still, may backfire by making what you aimed at your opponent turn on you (e.g. mistrust, paranoia, loss of control, stress).

Many of you may be surprised if I pick William Shakespeare – the person – as an example of invisibility at work. For someone who changed our way of presenting human nature, if not human nature itself, Shakespeare managed not to portray himself anywhere in his plays. This is a genius who managed to dissect the human mind perfectly. He created so many diverse, rich and detailed characters in his plays, unrivalled by any one since, yet he was able to remain undetectable as a person throughout his work.

Now consider any writer you could think of and if you examine their work, you are bound to find *traces* of their characters scattered throughout their work. With Shakespeare, considering the number of plays he wrote, if you attempt to deduce his personality from his plays, then be prepared to enter an endless maze which may eventually lead you to madness!

The stealth in Shakespeare's writing is one of the most underrated capabilities of his genius. The lesson from this example is that one can do so much, use as many strategic and tactical steps and plan with so much details, all this while still being invisible to his opponents (in the case of Shakespeare it's his readers).

Moving from the literary world and back to the world of manipulation, a potent combination of being invisible – working in the shadow – plus being underestimated is a very powerful and destructive way to break down your enemy. It generates in them a sense of paranoia, mistrust, impulsivity and stress to the point of mental and physical breakdown. It is especially potent in narcissistic individuals, who are more susceptible to those effects.

Guerrilla warfare is a good illustration of stealth and invisibility. Guerrilla tactics and warfare were employed throughout history. The approaches combine many tactics, but mainly slyness, unpredictability, covertness and deception.

They are based on uncoordinated, irregular, spontaneous, individual acts of sabotage, deception and ambush as opposed to direct altercation. Their ultimate objective is usually to destabilise the enemy through long, low-intensity confrontation. These tactics usually operate outside of constituted authority (e.g. from without) but can be used within enemy areas (i.e. from within).

In summary, avoid the urge and temptation to share your plans with others, or disclose (or brag) about what you are doing, or have done. Always keep the advantages of this strategy in mind and consider it an essential tactic in both the short and long term. If you uncover yourself after destroying a target, then in the future you will not be able to fight other opponents. So invisibility is a foundation for possible future wars and you should never reveal it, because all your future tactics depend on its availability.

14. Trust No One

"There are people I know who won't hurt me. I call them corpses."

-Randy K. Milholland

"An alliance with the powerful is never to be trusted."

-Fedrus

"(In war) no one is neutral."

-Winston Churchill

We all would love to think that trusting people is a virtue and a sign of goodness, and humanity. I would bet that reading the heading of this section, you have presumed that I would totally disagree with this. Well, in a way you are both wrong and right at the same time!

For me it is a matter of *context*. In this handbook it is *manipulation* and not *all aspects of life* (e.g. friendship, love, family). If you spend your life trusting no one, then that would be a sad and a miserable life, as from Darwinian evolutionary prospective and as human beings, companionship and trust are inherent necessities within our matrix.

You have to remember that this is a handbook on the art of manipulation and not a guide to the way you ought to live your life. Its application should be confined to manipulative environment and not your entire life. Trust, goodness, kindness, love, righteousness, compassion, decency etc. are all wonderful things, which enrich our lives and give us sense of fulfilment. So, I definitely urge you to enrich the quality of your life by adopting these great and amazing notions and virtues.

I will now go back to the concept of "trust in the context of the manipulation war" and remind you again of the initial step in this war, which is planning. We emphasised the idea of a meticulous and thorough scanning of your environment prior to finalising your manipulation plan. If you spend effort and time doing that then you can find a middle ground as far the issue of trust is concerned (i.e. whom to deem as trustworthy versus untrustworthy).

It is up to your surrounding circumstances and purposes when and who to trust. As I have been advocating the principle of simplicity as an advantage tactically and strategically, in my opinion, after looking at your environment, you should not trust anyone who is involved either directly or indirectly in your planning environment and surroundings (your field of operation).

The battlefield of the manipulation war is a theatre, and everyone is wearing a mask and a camouflage and, in a way, playing their part as actors. It is *in this environment* that adopting the principle of "trust no one" would be the wise thing to do. As Winston Churchill said, in war, "no one is neutral." I will add to this famous quote by saying that people's trust is fickle and alliances change depending on who is winning and what's in it for each individual in term of potential gain.

So for the purpose of this handbook which aims for you to wage an invisible manipulation war, where you are the warrior and only leader, trusting any party in the "game zone" is likely to be a mistake.

It is extremely hard for us as human beings to keep quiet and even harder to restrain ourselves from forging an alliance with a person or people who appear to have the same goal or common enemy as ourselves. It is this short sighted view or illusion which many of us employ, either out of fear of the enemy, seeking comfort by knowing that "We are not alone," or by thinking that an alliance would give us an advantage or a benefit against our opponent. These common tactics are used by many, and although they might work sometimes, on the whole their potential for harm is far more likely.

In this individualistic time, as we often said, we have to adapt. The ideal modern manipulation war requires secrecy, stealth and having enough individualistic skills to equip you to wage your invisible war alone, and as many times as the situation necessitates.

As an anticipatory tactic, there is the likelihood that you will face many enemies, and once you get rid of one, you may have to move to the next target. By trusting a person or group of people, who may have served you in conquering and manipulating your first opponent, it is extremely *unlikely* that they will share your views about your second, third, etc. opponents.

This "conflict of interest," which may emerge after few wars, is a recipe for your demise. You have parted with an essential element, which is your independence and in the process, you have revealed your secrets and intentions, relinquishing control and placing your fate in the hand of others from the same environment you're in (e.g. a firm, a company, a college)

This is an error which could have many undesirable consequences, such as that you may become the manipulated party by the individual you trusted with your mission and strategy. Worse still is that everything you have achieved and all the planning you have invested time and effort may be destroyed. This in turn renders you exposed for all to see by the trusted individual, if they deem you unnecessary, an obstacle to their own goals, or even if a simple disagreement occurs amongst you.

So no matter how or what your initial impression about an individual in term of trustworthiness is, think of the long term and anticipate every scenario which may happen in the future. Put simply, and to avoid all the above risks, insecurity and headaches, adopting the axiom "trust no one" in the context of the manipulation game would be the wise thing to do.

In summary, the aim of this handbook is to win the manipulation war by depending on yourself alone, adapting reliable tactics, being invisible throughout the process and anticipating that in these individualistic modern times you are most likely to have to face more than one opponent. *Trusting others* may initially appear like a good idea, especially in the short term, but in the long run it could turn out to be one of the biggest mistakes you make.

15. Prepare for Deception

"It is a double pleasure to deceive the deceiver."

-French Proverb

"It is a tribute to the humanity of ordinary people that
horrible acts must be camouflaged in a thicket of deceptive
words like 'security,' 'peace,' 'freedom,' 'democracy,' the
'national interest' in order to justify them."
-Howard Zinn

"In war, truth is the first casualty."
-Aeschylus

"All warfare is based on deception."
-Sun Tzu

Some of you may be surprised that I kept this tactic at the bottom of
the list, especially as almost all great authorities and minds in the field
of war rate it high on their list. That is not an underestimation on my
part, and I hope once you have read this section you will understand
my reason for placing it down the order. Also, remember that the
chronological order of the sections is *not based* on their importance. It
is done merely to help the subject matter flow smoothly.

Deceive (from the Latin *decipere*) is defined by The Oxford dictionary
as:

1. Deliberately mislead into believing something false.
2. (Of a thing) give a mistaken impression.

Let's be honest, how many of us do not use this in its proper meaning nearly every day? Almost the majority of us deceive in our daily interaction, even in the tiniest of ways. We do our best to give a favourable impression about ourselves. We sometime justify our action by using phrases such as, "White lies," or "Trying to be nice," or "I didn't want to hurt him/her." But, no matter how we rationalise it, it is still deception.

The fabric of our society is built on deception; we each *mislead* or *give a mistaken impression*, and as I said defend it morally by convincing ourselves, consciously or unconsciously, that it is justified. No matter if you branded it "big" or "small," "innocent" or "malicious," one could argue that it is still the same, because the underlying principle, ethic or whichever term you prefer to use, still carries a deceitful foundation.

One thing's for sure, to master the game of manipulation you have to build a big part of your strategic and tactical planning on deception. Remember that essentially you are dealing with a person for whom deception is a major part of their character. Playing nice (honest) does not work, and being sincere with these people does not work, either. In fact, they are counterproductive and you might as well concede defeat if you plan to be nice. The trick is to *appear* to be nice, to deceive these people into thinking that you are what *you want them* to think you are and not what you *truly* are!

I can guarantee you that there has not been a battle or confrontation in human history that has not used deception as an essential component in its conduct, and that even goes for the holiest of Holy Wars.

Tactically, deception is a great weapon to have at your disposal. It is extremely effective, secretive, misleading and has the potential to create chaos in a short period of time. Like almost all the strategic components we talked about, I am afraid that, once again, stealth is a must; otherwise you risk exposure and if that happens, then the damage could be irreversible and costly.

So let us now talk about a deceptive tactic which is extremely useful in obtaining information, infiltrating the enemy and eventually manipulating them. You will perhaps be surprised to know that the tactic is basically playing nice, or more accurately *deceiving* playing nice.

We have mentioned the importance of your body language combined with your verbal communication is in serving you to give whatever impression you wish, and also in deciphering your enemy, especially if you look at their non-verbal communication. Combine the previously mentioned tactics with another tactic, which is listening, (i.e. deceptive communication + deceptive listening) and the result can hardly fail to make you "appear" nice. Once people think you're nice, they will start to trust you. It is from there on that you could start using them to obtain sensitive, confidential information and even planting physical evidence.

Let's take the latter, planting physical evidence, as an example. If you combine listening, with submissive verbal and non-verbal communication (just to name a few methods); you could appear nice, even angelic, depending on your skills. Once you give this impression, automatically people will start to trust you. This in turn gives you the privilege to infiltrate their physical and emotional space.

If you are in a firm and want to implicate your enemy in theft for example, you can easily plant evidence, by taking important documents from one person and placing them on another person's desk. If you're good at deception, you would have appeared nice to all parties and therefore trusted by all. If that is the case, then indirect rumours or giving clues indirectly could achieve your goal and implicate your target. You could achieve all that while no one suspects a thing about you: the kind, listening and caring person!

It may sound too good to be true but the fact is that deception works. In the above example, combining (listening, communication, rumours) is guaranteed to obtain you results, if done appropriately. The only obstacle to achieving this is you and you alone. If you think it is complicated (remember this word does not exist in our vocabulary), and allow fears and doubt to take over, then you are asking for failure. Just keep in mind that all our tactics, if applied properly, are discreet and that failure is not the end, as you will still remain invisible.

By now, I don't think I need to tell you that you must anticipate deception and indeed expect it from anyone in your environment. No matter how nice a person may appear, stick to your rule of "trust no one" and remember that whether it is a company, a college, a factory or anything else, it is still a theatre and everyone is acting their part. So be self-reliant, think with your brain, don't be emotional, stay calm and under the radar and always remember your mission.

In summary, I hope that you noticed two things. First of all, that deception works and is "a must" in the war of manipulation as it gets results. Secondly, that this tactic basically is a combination of the many approaches we have mentioned previously. The main goal being, to make people trust you and give the impression you want to give, according to *your rules* and control. Also, be careful and anticipate deception from anyone and everyone and know how to prevent it and counteract it.

16. Know When to Stop, Redefine Failure and Learn from it to Move Forward

"If you have made mistakes, even serious ones, there is always another chance for you. What we call failure is not the falling down but the staying down."

-Mary Pickford

"A good general not only sees the way to victory, he also knows when victory is impossible."

-Polybius

"He who knows when he can fight and when he cannot will be victorious."

-Sun Tzu

Although we have insisted so far on the "don't give up" attitude and avoiding defeatist thinking, sometimes, in the midst of the game of manipulation, circumstances and luck could conspire against you. Stubbornness and tenacity do not work and most likely will give you away and expose you to the enemy. Once this happens, then you're an easy target, especially when you consider that one of the main objectives of this handbook is to operate alone and potentially against many opponents.

Just remember that throughout our discussion, all the strategic approaches could be deployed in secret, with you being undetectable, therefore even if you are forced to stop the war, nothing will happen in terms of retaliation by your opponent, because they are unaware that you are the mastermind behind the attacks.

That in itself is an advantage, because even if your opponents noticed that the attacks have stopped, a sense of paranoia and suspiciousness of everyone around them will surely happen; especially as the narcissist has issues with trust.

So even in retreat there are positives. Your enemy will be mentally occupied with thinking about the likely source of the attacks. That is to your benefit, as the longer they remain in this state, the weaker mentally and physically they will become. So once you are able to scan your environment again and feel ready to restart the battle, the dynamics will have changed, not only because you will have had time to implement new strategies, learned from your previous experience, but also your opponent will be weaker, full of doubt, paranoia and overall an easier target to manipulate and break down. In fact you could use this time to study your enemy's tactics and even use them. An example from ancient times is that of Scipio who studied Hannibal's tactics and brilliantly devised some of his own to defeat the once *invincible* Hannibal.

Another way to look at what we term *failure* was put very well by John Keats when he said, "don't be discouraged by a failure. It can be a positive experience. Failure is, in a sense, the highway to success, in as much as every discovery of what is false leads us to seek earnestly after what is true, and every fresh experience points out some form of error which we shall afterwards carefully avoid."

The above is a good lesson of a bigger philosophy which I hope that you have learnt by now, in that it is always easy to look at the negative side of a situation. To a certain extent, this is an outlook in the majority of people (it has an evolutionary *survival* purpose), but it is those few people who can look at the whole picture and take the negative – and more importantly the positive – from what appears as a failure, who are the winning breed and the successful leaders. So, logically speaking, there is no such thing as a complete failure or a complete success. It is a matter of percentages and the way you look at and read the situation.

If you find yourself faced with failure and do what the majority of us tend to do, which is "Do your best to forget the experience" or "Put it behind you," both of which are types of avoidance, then you have wasted a valuable source of information, and in the process, failed to learn from the experience. This subsequently, leads to failure to grow as a human being emotionally and intellectually (i.e. gain wisdom). The thing to do is to face failure, examine it and learn from its consequences.

In summary, the word *failure* in the game of manipulation does not have to have a negative connotation. On the contrary, you could use this experience to your advantage by resting, regrouping, rethinking and inducing a sense of paranoia and mistrust in your opponent. However, the biggest advantage of what is labelled as a "failure" is the opportunity to gain valuable wisdom.

17. Enlisting the Services of *Unaware* Devoted Allies

"The really great people are the ones who know how to make
the little people feel great."

-Ashleigh Brilliant

"To write well, express yourself like common people,
but think like a wise man. Or, think as wise men
do, but speak as the common people do."

-Aristotle

"Great people give inspiration by their
deeds. They lead by examples.
Common people always emulate them."

-Sam Veda

Before you jump to any conclusion, our goals remain the same: working alone and be an invisible manipulator. However, that does not mean that you can't have loyal allies wherever the battle is taking place. The trick is to be able to recruit these *loyal allies* without their awareness that they have been enlisted!

One of the greatest skills you can possess is the ability to make people do what you want, without them realising it. Moreover, you want them to volunteer, even be delighted to do so. Basically, your aim is to recruit loyal, devoted, volunteered and *unaware* individuals, in your battle against manipulation.

By now, if you have read this far, you should have a rough idea of the ways and steps to achieve this goal. We have devoted many sections on how to leave a good impression on people by methods such as listening and using your nonverbal gestures.

You may not know it, but the fact is that roughly 70% of the impression you leave on people is made within the first four minutes of meeting them, with the first glance being the most crucial. Now combine this enormously important knowledge with the skills regarding making a positive impression, and *make the most of those first four minutes*, so that they bring you close to achieving the goal of this section.

I want you to always consider this when you are meeting new people or joining an organisation of any kind. It is the people you leave with a good impression, *even if you hardly see them*, that are your potential future loyal allies.

By now, you ought to know that human beings are superficial and emotional creatures and if you are able to exploit these aspects, then you have already recruited your soldiers. Thus, you will still be able to be invisible and independent with an army behind you, who are devoted to you without being asked to do so.

So make sure to win over as many individuals as possible in any setting for a potential future conflict by remembering the importance of first impression and the strategic approaches which make you appear nice to people. The more unaware recruits you have, the more likely the strategic step we mentioned so far will be easier to execute.

As I have said, this strategic approach does not contradict our main philosophies, as long as you remember and do the following:

- Leaving a good impression and winning people over does not mean you befriend them or get too close to them. You can achieve the favourable impression in the first few minutes and then just keep reinforcing it by simple gestures (e.g. a daily smile, stopping for a quick *listening* chitchat and basically being nice).

- "Trust no one" still applies, but that does not mean that you show it; as we discussed earlier, the greatest skill is to give the impression or illusion that you are *both* trustworthy and trusting at the same time.

- Your invisibility and anonymity are still a crucial part of your tactics, and getting people to like you does not mean that this has to change. On the contrary, as we have said throughout, people love quiet, non-threatening listening individuals.

- Anticipation and awareness of the unpredictability of people is still a fact. Loyalty is never unconditional or total, so keep scanning the environment and do not assume loyalty is absolute.

Now that we covered the fact that you are able to recruit people to your side without compromising your philosophy and main goals, we move onto the practicality of having loyal allies as a strategic component.

Once war is waged and you're in the middle of a manipulation and conflict, you will need all your skills and resources at your disposal. Your *unaware* allies might make all the difference, in fact; they might even do all the work for you without being asked to.

Here is where a bit of social psychology knowledge would offer an explanation for this phenomenon. If people *like you* and have a favourable impression of you, even though they didn't or don't truly know you, they will act emotionally to defend you, especially if in the scale of likeability, you are rated higher than your opponents. If that is the case (and is usually is, if you're up against a true manipulator), then they will act as your defenders, even though you didn't ask them to. This army could wage the war against your enemy, all by itself, even up to the point of defeating them.

Another interesting fact from group social psychology is that actually having a "superficial favourable first impression based relationship" in group setting may be far more effective than a "deeper relationship."

This is because if a group has a favourable *superficial* impression about you, they will tend to *fill-in* all the unknown aspect about your character with favourable assumptions. On the other hand, if the group got to know you at a deeper level, then emotional factors plus realistic information about you comes into play. In this case, the "idealised version" of you (*perfect you*), which is likely in a superficial setting, will be replaced by a "realistic version" of you (*human you*). This is why people often advice you never to meet your idols or heroes. Once you do that, you often discover how *human* they are, and the idealised version is replaced by a realistic, often disappointing one.

The strategic goal of recruiting unaware allies is an ideal scenario and, unlike other tactics, you cannot and should not rely on it in your planning, because it is unpredictable. Adopt the attitude that if it works then it is all well and good and if it doesn't, then you have enough skills to accomplish your mission, plus your philosophies and strategies are not dependent on other people's loyalty as a necessary requirement.

A common mistake made by many people once they join any establishment of any kind such as company, political party or any other organisation, is that they try very hard to please the hierarchy (e.g. the bosses).

In fact, the aim should be to start bottom-up, meaning trying to please the little people (i.e. the lower in term of rank or status) first, such as the janitors, the security guards, and the manual and office workers. It is these people who will eventually be of more use to you once you're in conflict. They could be your silent soldiers, defending you "behind your back" without being asked to do so.

This is because these individuals, unlike the people at the top, usually tend to have no hidden or competitive agendas. They are emotional, and if you are able to show them genuine respect and leave a favourable impression on them, then they are very likely to be on your side if a war ensues. They will serve you, enabling you to achieve and apply your tactics much more easily and in a faster way and shorter length of time.

Do not underestimate the power of the *little (common) people*, as all major revolutions throughout history have depended on them; from the French Revolution to the rise and fall of the Communist Soviet Union.

In summary, if you play your cards right, then you may be able to recruit people to serve you in your war against the enemy. The trick is to use your skills and strategies to achieve this without the recruits being aware that they are recruited! Do not underestimate the power of the regular people, regardless of their status, as a potential winning weapon against your opponent. Just remember the importance of that first impression and the use of nonverbal communication skills as tools for indirect recruitment.

18. Relaxation and Stress

"This art of resting the mind and the power of dismissing from it all care and worry is probably one of the secrets of energy in our great men."
-Captain J. A. Hadfield

"When we are unable to find tranquility within ourselves, it is useless to seek it elsewhere."
-Francois de La Rochefoucauld

"If a man insisted always on being serious, and never allowed himself a bit of fun and relaxation, he would go mad or become unstable without knowing."
-Herodotus

Let us start this section by a brief scientific description about the physiology of stress. The benefit of this knowledge will become apparent once we discuss its usefulness in the game of manipulation. So for those of you who are not scientifically *enthusiastic*, you have to bear with me and I will do my best to keep it simple; after all, we don't want you to get stressed!

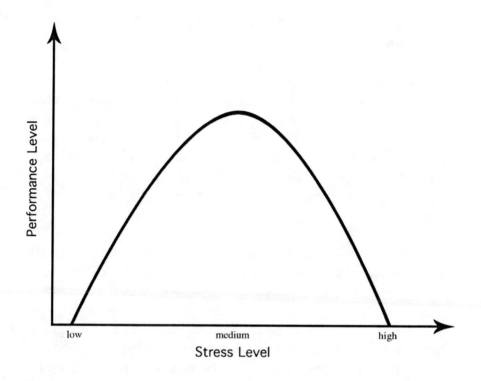

The above figure shows what is referred to as the Yerkes-Dodson Curve (for the sake of simplicity, let's call it the Stress Curve). The principle behind it implies that to a certain point, a specific amount of stress is healthy, useful, and even beneficial. This usefulness can be translated not only to performance but also to one's health, concentration and well-being.

Stress response is often essential for success. We see this commonly in situations such as sporting events, academic pursuits and even in many creative and social activities. As stress levels increase, so does performance. However, this relationship between increased stress and increased performance does not continue indefinitely.

As shown in Figure 1, The Stress Curve illustrates that, up to a point, stress or arousal can increase performance. Conversely, when stress exceeds one's ability to cope with it, this overload contributes to diminished performance, inefficiency, loss of concentration, exhaustion and even health problems (high blood pressure, risk of stroke, low immunity, etc.).

Now that the science bit and background are done with, let us move on to the practical application of this knowledge in our game of manipulation. In a way, this tactic is unique compared to the others as it is less aggressive and in some ways complements the others. It is perhaps also fitting to include it at the end of the book with the main focus of calming things down and informing you when to slow down. However like the other tactics, you can either apply it to yourself or against your opponent.

In terms of benefit, it informs you when to slow down or even pause. If you find yourself reaching the peak of the curve, it means that you ought to slow down because if you continue, you will reach the exhaustion stage (*breaking point*). So no matter how strong or enthusiastic you are, remember that we all have a breaking point. Even if things are going your way, but you feel the effort and work is beginning to drain you mentally or physically, then you should stop. Once you do that, you can recharge your batteries by relaxing, using whichever method you prefer – spiritual, exercise, time off, hobbies, etc.

Throughout this handbook, we have focused on taking your time, being calm, overcoming negative emotions, attacking gradually and taking simple steps. All these measures are so that you don't peak too soon and reach the breaking point too fast. A major mistake a lot of people make is that they get so excited, especially once they can feel that they are "almost there," that they start to push themselves to the limit, but this attitude may backfire. Remember that the manipulation game is a marathon and not a sprint, so curb your enthusiasm no matter what you feel and think (remembering to let your thinking guide your feelings or emotions), focus and slow down.

Now we move onto how to use this understanding of stress physiology, as a tool against your opponent. Firstly, you could use this awareness as a guide to when to start, strike or increase the attack on your enemy. An opponent on a higher level on the curve will be much easy to breakdown, as the amount of stress required is far less than if they are at a lower point. So again, take your time and once you see your opponent exhibiting a high level of stress, that's the time for you to make your move.

Secondly, do not underestimate the power of creating little hassles, as each one could push your enemy a step further toward the exhaustion stage. This *accumulative effect* could be a very powerful weapon; so for example, in an office, indirectly sending irritating e-mails, taking away pens or paper, causing an unsteady chair or spilling coffee "accidentally" on your opponent, may sound childish and trivial, but, I can assure you that all these little upsets or hassles, have an accumulative effect and are a very useful way to break down your opponent.

Each hassle, biologically speaking, results in the release of stress hormones, and it is these hormones which are the fuel pushing the person up the stress curve and toward an eventual breaking point. How many times have you witnessed a person "losing it" over what appears to be a trivial matter, e.g. your boss throwing a major temper tantrum because he can't find his pen? It is simplistic to think that this incident caused the tantrum, because it is the accumulative effect of many hassles and stressors which are the real reason. The pen incident was merely "The straw that broke the camel's back!"

A final method by which you could deploy this knowledge involves deception, and it is particularly useful if you are faced with two opponents at the same time. If you are able to notice when one opponent is on the verge of breakdown, almost reaching the stress peak, try to put the other person in a position where he or she carries out the final push or *the last straw*.

For example, if at work you are able to spot the opponent on the verge, try to find a way to make them have a direct or indirect contact with the other opponent which will likely to result in a hassle for the first opponent, keeping in mind that even a very trivial matter could do the job. If this happens, then the two opponents will clash – if they are of the same rank – or the opponent with the lower rank will breakdown and in the process make the other opponent – of the higher rank – appear bad or nasty in front of others.

The above are just few ways on how to utilise the Stress Curve knowledge and I am sure that you can come up with other ways, depending on your environment and setting, to achieve results; backed by solid, sound and good planning as the foundation for a successful strategy.

In summary, a simple knowledge about the biology of stress could be of great practical use both to strengthen you and weaken your opponents. This tactic is less aggressive than the other ones, complements them, is easy to apply, is very subtle, requires little effort and can be used as a monitor to assess both your resources and those of your enemy.

In Conclusion

The word *manipulate* means: to control, influence or mislead. In today's individualistic society we are faced with manipulation and manipulators almost every day and in different settings, whether at work, in the media, in businesses or in politics.

The manipulator's mind-set and thinking is different from that of "normal" individuals. It is preoccupied with power, success, ingrained beliefs of uniqueness and a sense of entitlement. The manipulator is exploitative, spiteful, arrogant and takes advantage of others to achieve their own goals. Narcissistic individuals ("real" manipulators), lack empathy and a willingness to recognise the feelings of others and is actually envious of them.

When we are faced with such an adversary we have two choices, either to be submissive and allow them to achieve their desires, or to fight back.

Fighting back should not be a random response based on the heat of the moment, or on our emotions. The manipulator's task becomes easy if we revert to these actions. They thrive on our misfortunes, emotional pain and suffering. For them to build up their fragile self confidence and self-esteem, they attempt to crush ours. To fight back, we have to adopt different approaches.

There is an ongoing war, but unlike the old traditional ones, this war is waged by individuals. No longer are strength in numbers and artillery the key to victory. The modern "manipulation war" requires strategic planning, tactics and focus. It is an invisible war and victory is achieved through subtlety and understanding of the mind-set and thinking of your opponents.

Luckily for us, we have moved forward in many fields and our understanding of the way a manipulator functions has expanded.

It is this knowledge that we need to update and modify in order to win the war of manipulation and have the ability to manipulate the manipulators.

We have to plan ahead using diverse strategic planning and tactical manoeuvres derived from various fields such as psychology, philosophy, history, business, technology, spirituality, politics, military, sociology and science. I strongly believe that the era of speciality (i.e. knowledge in one field alone — for example politics) is an obstacle for any person or group trying to progress. This is the era of diversity in knowledge, lateral thinking and innovation. It is this modern outlook that forms the base for our manipulation planning.

As we have already said, society's structure has changed. We, in modern times, are individualistic creatures, more so than any time in history. Many of us are egocentric and self-centred. We all think that we are leaders, whether we want to admit it or not; it is the norm rather than the exception. This is almost a complete reversal of society's attitude centuries ago. This change should alert us to be self-reliant, independent, disciplined and acquire the necessary knowledge of the tactics mentioned earlier, so that we are equipped to apply them with stealth and in a structured way against our manipulative opponent.

The strategic approaches in this book pave the way to targeting manipulative individuals. All the strategic approaches make use of the fact that to a certain extent we are able to predicate the manipulative, malicious and narcissistic individual's behaviour. It is this important factor in their mind-set that constitutes the main strategic advantage in our game of manipulation.

It is extremely important to understand how the manipulative mind works and once you are able to achieve this objective, you can move to the strategic steps. Here, also one must understand the basic idea behind each approach and only once this is achieved, one can embark on the war with confidence, belief and determination to win the battle.

Of all the approaches mentioned in this handbook, one of the most important is to target the enemy's emotions. The narcissist (manipulator) may appear very strong and it is by targeting their emotional weaknesses in a strategic and tactical way that this apparent strength will vanish and the true narcissistic fragile, weak self will appear.

Although the above approach is crucial, nevertheless the other strategic steps should not be neglected and one should view all the strategic approaches mentioned as interrelated and complementing each other. Only by applying a carefully designed strategy with all its components, and with the addition of the other various tactics and approaches mentioned in this book, can you reach your ultimate goal and win the game or war of manipulation.

References

- American Psychiatric Association. *Diagnostic and Statistical Manual of Mental Disorders 4th Edition (DSM-IV)*. American Psychiatric Association. Washington, DC.1994.

- Bear MF., Connors BW. & Paradiso. *Neuroscience: Exploring the Brain*. Second Edition. Lippincot Williams & Wilkins. A Wolters Kluwer Company. USA. 2001

- Beck AT. *Cognitive Therapy and Emotional Disorders* by Beck AT. International Universities Press, New York, NY. 1976.

- Berry LL. *On Great Service: A Framework for Action*. The Free Press, New York. 1995

- Bierman J & Smith C. *The Battle of Alamein: Turning Point, World War II*. Viking Adult. 2002.

- Bloom H. *Genius: A Mosaic of One Hundred Exemplary Creative Minds*. Warner Books, New York, NY. 2002

- Bowles N. *Nixon's Business: Authority and Power in Presidential Politics (The Presidency and Leadership)*. Texas A&M University Press, College Station. 2005.

- Clavell J. *The Art of War: Sun Tzu*. Revised Edition 2006. A Mobius Book.

- Collins JL. *Good to Great*. Harper Collins. New York, NY. 2001.

- Cottrell L. *Hannibal: Enemy of Rome* .De Capo Press, NY. 1992.

- Deming WE. *The New Economics for Industry, Government, Education*. Cambridge: Massachusetts Institute of Technology. 1993

- Freud A. *The ego and the mechanisms of defence*. Hogarths Press. London. 1936.

- Green P. *Alexander the Great and the Hellenistic Age*. Orion Books. 2007.

- Gelder M, Harrison P, Cowen P. *Short Oxford Textbook of Psychiatry*. Fifth Edition. Oxford University Press. 2006.

- Hausman C. *Lies We Live By: Defeating Doubletalk and Deception in Advertising, Politics, and the Media*. Routledge, New York, NY. 2000

- Holmes J. *Narcissism: Ideas in Psychoanalysis*. Icon Books. 2001.

- Kernberg OF. *Borderline Conditions and Pathological Narcissism*. Jason Aronson, New York. 1975.

- Leistyna P. *Presence Of Mind: Education And The Politics Of Deception*. Westview Press, Colorado, USA. 1998

- Machiavelli N, Constantine P, and Ascoli AR. *The Prince*. Modern Library Classics. (Paperback - Feb 5, 2008).

- Moen RD & Nolan TN. *Process Improvement*. Quality Progress, 1987: 62-68.

- Oxford University Press. *The Oxford Dictionary*. Oxford University Press. 2008.

- Porter ME. On Competition. Harvard Business Review Books. Boston, MA. 1998.

- Robert NA. *Planning and Control Systems: A Framework for Analysis*. Boston, Division of Research, Graduate School of Business Administration, Harvard University. 1965.

- Schroeder RG. *Operations Management*. New York, NY. McGraw Hill. 1985

- Spear ST. *Learning to Lead at Toyota*. Harvard Business Review. 2004 May: 78-91.

- Stevenson RL. *Strange Case of Dr. Jekyll & Mr. Hyde*. Everyman's Library.1996.

- Weatherford J. *Genghis Khan and the Making of Modern World*. Random House Inc. 2005

- Wilde O. *The Picture of Dorian Gray*. Wilder Publication, US. 2007.

- Yerkes, R. M., & Dodson, J. D. The relation of strength of stimulus to rapidity of habit-formation. *Journal of Comparative Neurology and Psychology*. 1908; 18, 459-482.

LaVergne, TN USA
29 December 2009

168442LV00006B/1/P